POWER & GLORY

Jimmy Page & Robert Plant

POWER & GLORY

Jimmy Page & Robert Plant

Chris Welch

ZOMBA BOOKS

ACKNOWLEDGEMENT

The author would like to thank Howard Mylett for his tireless assistance and enthusiasm.

First published in Great Britain in 1985 by Zomba Books,
Zomba House, 165–167 Willesden High Road, London
NW10 2SG, and in the United States of America by Cherry
Lane Books, Port Chester, NY 10573, New York, U.S.A.

©Chris Welch, 1985
ISBN 0 946391 74 2
First Edition

Production Services by Book Production Consultants,
Cambridge.

Typeset by Wenden Typesetting Services, Saffron Walden.
Printed by Bemrose Printing C.I.P., Derby.

Designed by Jim Reader
Cover Designed by Mark Lovell

PHOTOGRAPHERS CREDITS

Photographs courtesy of Barry Plummer, K. R. Butcher, Carl Dunn, Barrie Wentzell, Richard Brown, Paul Lockey, Hellerman, Russell Chambers, Brian Knapp, Hugh Jones, and Howard Mylett. Cover photos courtesy of Barry Plummer.

Whilst every effort has been made to trace and contact the photographers of all the pictures, in some cases it was impossible. The publishers apologise to any photographer who has not been credited.

Live Aid picture courtesy of Retna Pictures Ltd.

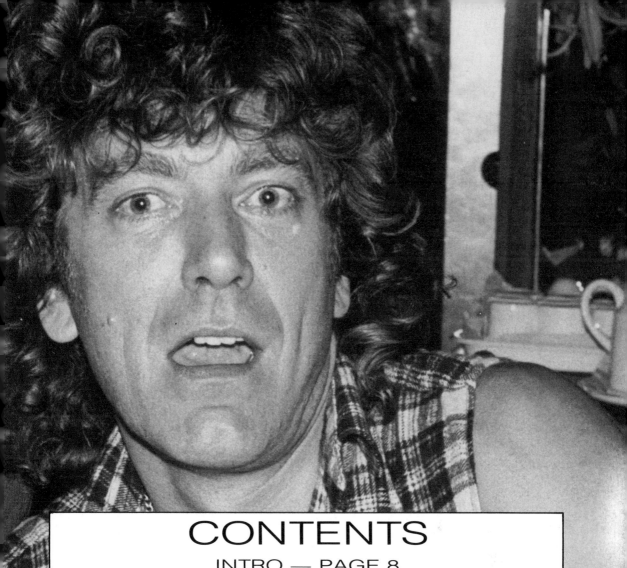

CONTENTS

A FAN'S EYE VIEW

Jimmy Page and Robert Plant are names that are synonymous with the seventies, but their careers span over twenty years in the music business, including twelve with one of the most successful rock bands of all time, Led Zeppelin. After much soul searching and musical exploration, the two men have now created separate and highly productive new ventures for the eighties. Both singer and guitarist are still travelling the world, performing new and vastly different music.

As a devoted follower of both musicians, I noted with pride the enthusiasm that greeted Jimmy Page when he returned to live performance for the first time since the break up of Led Zeppelin. Whenever he set foot on stage, whether for his solo spot during the ARMS charity show at London's Royal Albert Hall in September 1983, or with his new group, The Firm, a year later, the crowds welcomed him with a special affection reserved for the Master of Rock Guitar. When I saw The Firm, with Jimmy and Paul Rodgers, at the Odeon Hammersmith in December 1984, he proved himself ready to rock and not willing to rest on past, hard won laurels. It was a great 'home coming'.

The same sense of 'welcome back' applied when Robert Plant launched his own solo career. After Led Zeppelin split, in late 1980, Robert played in and around small pubs and clubs with a group called The Honeydrippers. Backed by an ever changing personnel he concentrated on old rock'n'roll and blues numbers, never intending the project to be interpreted as a permanent unit. He made several attempts to play down the importance of these events even cancelling one concert that advertised he was in the line-up, as the real reason for the gigs was that it gave him and his Midlands friends a chance to play together and have a good time, now that the pressure of sustaining Zeppelin was off.

He seemed to be edging his way back into the limelight but the death of John Bonham, drummer and personal friend, left him greatly distressed for a long time. After many changes (particularly where drummers were concerned), Robert settled down with a regular crew of musicians, and embarked on an American tour once he had two albums worth of material under his belt. He made a successful debut with his new band in the summer of 1983 and later played in Britain.

I went to see him play at the Brighton Centre in December that year and was fortunate to find he was still the same larger than life character; humorous, likeable and very good at putting people at their ease. He had none of the pretensions of a 'superstar'. Peter Grant, his old manager from Led Zep days, was visiting as well, and the old campaigners seemed to have a continuing respect for each other.

While Jimmy's performances with The Firm stayed with basic rock and harked back to some Zeppelin traditions, Robert's music utilised space age sounds, synthesisers, and thunderous bass and drums. Jimmy returned to the violin bow and laser beams for his performances: Robert had a more subdued, controlled stage image and his new songs called for softer passages; although his voice remained powerful and in control whatever the mood.

As a 'faceless fan' among the crowds, I still felt the same excitement at their concerts that I'd felt in the old days. Much has been written of the 'legacy' of Led Zeppelin including some harsh and unfair criticism from people who seem frustrated in their attempts to categorise the group, as, over the years, their music moved away from the simple 'heavy' vein to more exploratory and complex sounds. Events in the lives of the group members themselves also influenced the lyrics and musical direction of the band.

One vital factor has been the bond of friendship between the two men which had endured through thick and thin. They keep a close eye on each other's work although neither of them include Zeppelin numbers in their shows (even when Jimmy played 'Stairway To Heaven' at the ARMS concerts, he did it as an instrumental and wouldn't let anyone else sing lyrics which are so closely associated with Robert). Zeppelin influences still show through however, and Robert cannot resist adding those familiar vocal cries of 'Push, push' and 'Ooh yeah, ooh yeah' to his newest songs, while Jimmy's use of a violin bow on the electric guitar continues to be one of his most famous trade marks and his expert use of 'distortion' and sustained notes are sure fire crowd pleasers. His barrage of effects can sound like an air raid, or an electronic army marching into battle – the spectacle of Page wielding his neon-tipped bow inside a spinning pyramid of laser beams is pure Rock Theatre.

Jimmy and Robert are both wise enough to realise that Led Zeppelin made them. Both are justifiably proud of their past achievements, such as filling New York's Madison Square Garden to capacity for seven nights, but now that the Zeppelin dust has settled and time has marched on, Robert has spoken of wanting to become more accessible to the public and media. In doing so he has gained far more exposure and

● *A break in rehearsals, 1980.*

become prominent in mainstream pop music, promoting his songs with special videos. Significantly his first 'live' appearance in his new role on television was on BBC TV's *Top Of The Pops*, when his hit single 'Big Log' entered the charts.

There is always hope among fans that Page and Plant, whose lives have been so intertwined, will one day reunite. In fact, they already have. The occasions came when Jimmy played a solo on 'Sea Of Love', a track on The Honeydrippers' album. The cut was released as a single and went straight into the American charts. The song showed once again the natural affinity between Plant and Page, and the magic they always manage to generate.

America, the land which first accepted Led Zeppelin, has shown the swiftest appreciation for their present day activities. The MTV rock music channel showed a half hour version of The Firm's second night at London's Hammersmith Odeon and Robert has appeared on *Saturday Night Live*, the top US TV show, singing 'Santa Claus Is Coming To Town' accompanied by Stray Cats' guitarist Brian Setzer, one of Robert's favourite musicians.

In a burst of activity, Robert toured Australia, New Zealand, and Japan and was scheduled to tour America and England again in 1985. His third solo album *Shaken'n'Stirred*, on his own Es Parenza label, utilised guitar synthesisers and girl backing vocals, showing Robert's desire to advance while retaining his rock roots.

Today, Jimmy's reputation as a musical craftsman and Robert's as one of the finest singers of all time, remain intact and unsullied, and I, for one, eagerly look forward to each stage in their advancement. I keep an open mind and ever attentive ears!

Someone I feel can relate to my enthusiasm for the work of Plant and Page is rock journalist and critic Chris Welch. We have worked and researched together as much information as possble for this chronicle of their careers, going back to the mid-sixties when Robert was a struggling would be 'pop star', with a wealth of ideas but an uncertain future, and when Jimmy Page was a secret session man, even before his days with the legendary Yardbirds. It's a fascinating story which I hope you will enjoy – and of course, for Plant and Page in the eighties, the story has only just begun! HOWARD MYLET, Brighton, Sussex. June 1985.

CHAPTER ONE
"POWER AND GLORY"

When talents collide, the result can be an explosion of heat and energy. When Jimmy Page and Robert Plant met up in the band called Led Zeppelin the shock wave spread out over three decades of rock history. Both men have enjoyed careers before and beyond the phenomenon of Zeppelin but their names have become inextricably linked as composers, performers and showmen. When Led Zeppelin was at its peak as the world's premier rock band in the seventies, theirs indeed was the power and the glory.

The strutting figure of the bare-chested Plant, golden hair flowing over broad shoulders, singing like a Viking warrior, was matched by the frail but mysterious Page – dark eyed magician on the guitar – summoning powerful forces to aid their conquest and victories.

A fanciful picture but an enduring image and not so far from the truth. The princely partnership was celebrated on record, in photographs and on film, and reached its apogee with the song 'Stairway To Heaven', a moving medieval ballad. It was just one of many songs that the collaboration produced during a ten year period, but its haunting melody and evocative lyrics made it one of the most memorable compositions of the era, still played on radio when so much music of the seventies has been discarded and forgotten.

Led Zeppelin was not just a two man band. With John Paul Jones on keyboards and John Bonham on drums, they made a powerful, apparently invincible team whose exploits have become legendary. But it was the principals who provided much of the creative drive and the focal point for fans around the world, for in the hands of Plant and Page, and guided by their manager Peter Grant, Led Zeppelin became the most successful touring rock band to follow in the wake of The Beatles.

● LEFT: *Scrapin' a living.*
Jimmy at Earl's Court, 1975.

● *Beards were all the rage in 1970.*

were invariably sell outs attended by headlines and controversy.

They pushed forward the technological boundaries of the expanding rock movement: marathon two to three hour concerts (unheard of in the sixties), bigger and better PA systems, new production ideas on record, a bigger and better spectacle on stage. They were among the first to take truck loads of equipment on the road, with more sophisticated amplifiers, speakers and instruments to fill out the huge sports stadiums and arenas, as rock outgrew its breeding ground of small clubs and pubs. Even before Zeppelin, Jimmy Page had been quick to use such innovations as the fuzz box and wah wah pedal and would constantly experiment with effects units and unusual instruments. He would oversee Zeppelin's early use of the new laser technology, and projection screens which added an even larger dimension to Zeppelin's act.

This was window dressing on a grand scale, necessary when playing to the thousands of fans who flocked to every sell out show from New York to Tokyo but the root of their appeal lay in their basic simplicity and direct approach to audiences. There was no communication breakdown between Plant, Page and their fans. Robert in his blue jeans, clutching a trusty harmonica was essentially a man o'the people. Jimmy was more remote and mysterious, but there was always the feeling that Zeppelin was a people's band the one that wouldn't turn up on any old TV pop show, that wouldn't play by the media rules. Zeppelin fans didn't admire Plant and Page because they were hoodwinked by some spurious publicity campaign or adroit marketing. In fact during their launch period, there was a suspicion among the band that they were being ignored, by press, promoters and the music business in general.

When success came, first in America, and then swiftly back home in England, it was in the form of a popular choice with fans feeding off their own grapevine of information. In the late sixties, apart from the attention accorded to the drug habits of a few superstars, pop music and rock was generally ignored by the national press and TV while radio generally played only the most instantly accessible chart pop. It was the grassroots success of Zeppelin in turning on mass audiences (already titillated by the advent of Cream and the Jimi Hendrix Experience), that gave rock power and status.

The Zeppelin crew would never allow themselves to become groomed and polished pop stars in the old mould. They had seen too much of that at close hand and knew its debilitating effects on an artist. Both Jimmy and Robert might have had their heads stuffed full of curious notions at various stages of their development, but generally a sound common sense, wit and intelligence prevailed, making them, as much as is possible within a talent devouring industry, masters of their own destiny.

Both were from middle class family backgrounds, with no great dramas or upsets in their early lives.

Such achievement was based on sound musical roots and ability. For all their 'heavy' reputation, Jimmy and Robert have never come anywhere near the excesses of glam rock or heavy metal. Their work together was based on the blues, folk and rock'n'roll and it was essentially their love of music and the freedom to play what they felt, that brought them together. It is the same motivation that keeps them hard at work today.

It was the shared interest in the blues tradition that led to their creating the musical dialogues that helped bond them as a team. Robert's voice, armed with astonishing range and power, was able to match in whoops and yells the swoops and howls of Page's guitar, whipping up an erotic frenzy. It's a device, the 'call and response', that goes back beyond the roots of country blues into church music, and Plant and Page gave it a whole new potency. This aspect of their work was celebrated on 'Good Times Bad Times' the first song on their first album together, Led Zeppelin, which was released in early 1969.

There were few more exciting spectacles in rock than Plant and Page blasting through 'You Shook Me', 'Dazed And Confused', 'Communication Breakdown', 'I Can't Quit You Baby', 'How Many More Times', 'Whole Lotta Love', 'The Lemon Song', 'Trampled Underfoot', 'Kashmir' and 'Achilles Last Stand' – just some of the outstanding songs from their eight studio albums. Fans in Britain, Europe, America, Japan and Australia were all mesmerised by the collective force of Zeppelin. Their albums sold millions, golds and platinums being awarded by an awestruck record industry like confetti. Their tours – gruelling and seemingly endless in the early days –

They were essentially from the generation of kids growing up in post-war England whose enthusiasm and desire to channel a natural spirit of rebellion to some sort of creative use gave rise to an army of 'beat groups'. They were the happy breed who tumbled out of the grammar and secondary schools in the late fifties and early sixties, who had just kissed goodbye to the threat of national service as army conscripts, and knew nothing of such concepts as 'inflation', 'unemployment' or 'recession'. They were expected to be accountants, engineers, draftsmen, civil servants, clerks or factory workers. Instead they became Kinks, Animals, Beatles, Stones, Hollies, Yardbirds and Zeppelins. Then, instead of being made redundant, they became (many of them) millionaires.

They rarely had time to dwell on such ironies, or the fact that never was so much parental advice ignored so frequently and so profitably. Jimmy , Robert, and many more plunged straight from school into the lives of itinerant musicians, and have known no other form of existence since. For them the norm has always been irregular hours, sleeping and eating according to the dictates of tour schedules, and burning the candle at both ends and in the middle. Long ago they cheerfully exchanged the tyranny of clocking on for the grind of life on the road. Despite the toll on health, life and limb, this was a generation hooked on gig-

● *Fancy finger work at Earl's Court.*

ging – they know they can never give it up.

It was early exprience on the road in a variety of bands that gave Jimmy and Robert their grounding and experience. That, combined with the sudden removal of all restrictions and frustrations, made Led Zeppelin such an explosive force.

Robert was a grammar school boy from the Midlands who would have been a chartered accountant – that is if he hadn't been lured away from his mapped out career by a love of pop music and the blues. He began singing with a variety of local groups around the thriving Birmingham scene, with names like the Black Snake Moan and Crawling King Snakes. He quickly developed a reputation as a powerful singer, and charismatic front man. He recorded his first single with a group called Listen and at the age of eighteen followed it with two solo singles. He regularly fronted his own band called The Band Of Joy which at times included his drumming friend John Bonham. When they split up he worked with another great blues enthusiast, the late Alexis Korner.

Jimmy Page meanwhile had grown up in the London suburbs, at Feltham, near London Airport. He led a normal childhood, singing, taking part in school sports and studying art. But from the moment his parents bought him a guitar for his twelfth birthday, his life became wrapped up in music. The simple acquisition of a guitar would unlock whole new worlds. The boy who left school with five 'O' levels and the prospect of becoming a laboratory assistant, instead joined his first rock band, Neil Christian and the Crusaders. From then on, with a few hitches, he would become a working, professional musician, whose speed at mastering the guitar and imagination when it came to playing rock'n'roll made him the first of a rare breed – the young British session musician.

Some five years older than Robert Plant, Jimmy Page was able to pack in much more activity and experience before their paths crossed. Throughout the early sixties he built up an underground reputation as the guitarist whose sound was just right: the older session men, weaned on jazz, couldn't, or wouldn't, get the right earthy sound that producers needed; the younger lead guitar players with 'one hit wonder' bands couldn't get it together fast enough in the studio to make their next hit. Invariably, Page was

the man they called in. Sometimes, as Jimmy would describe it later, simply as 'insurance'.

Eventually he tired of studio session work and yearned to be out on the road once again, which eventually brought him into the Yardbirds working alongside another fine guitarist, Jeff Beck. When the Yardbirds fell apart, Page then seized the opportunity to put a band together. It was in his quest for a singer and through the recommendation of a mutual friend that he was led to Robert Plant. Page was astounded when he first heard Robert sing and couldn't believe that he had not been snapped up before. Robert was similarly honoured to be invited by the already legendary Page to be part of his new team, and he in turn recommended a drummer; his old friend John Bonham.

Friendship grew quickly between Plant and Page. Their personalities; a complex mixture of strength and softness, outward humour and inward brooding; both challenged and complemented each other. There was no rivalry for honours. Each had their job to do within Zeppelin, their newly formed creation. Robert's own experiments and flirtations with West Coast psychedelia were shelved, and Jimmy's journeyman approach to rock was set aside. Their aims and ideas became focused on each helping the other to achieve new heights. All those nights in smokey backrooms had prepared them for the big stage Zeppelin presented. Success would take them all on a wild ride with excesses and abuse but in terms of man hours, they probably spent many more riding planes and reading books than they ever did smashing up hotel rooms or groping groupies. Such peaks and troughs were separated by the long, straight line of achievement.

By the end of the seventies the pair were burdened by their reputation and the high expectations of the fans. In a sense they were trapped and their dilemma was not alieviated by the sneering scorn of new generations of critics who saw them as anachronisms. Nevertheless the band were prepared to carry on, to give the fans what they wanted in concerts and on tours, and to continue to search for inspiration in the studio. They had survived a number of personal disasters and calamites, but then came the final blow. John Bonham died after a heavy drinking bout and the tragedy signalled the end of Led Zeppelin.

It took five years for Plant and Page to recover, pick up the pieces and rebuild their careers. Robert was first off the mark with new albums, new music and a new image. Jimmy Page involved himself in studio projects, writing and recording film music before coming back to 'live' performance with his band, The Firm, at the end of 1984. Both men kept in touch during this period, exchanging confidences and encouragement, and Jimmy played on Robert's *Honeydrippers Volume One* album.

One day their talents might reunite on a more permanent basis, however now is the time to look back at the music and events that brought them together in the first place.

CHAPTER TWO

JIMMY PAGE:
THE EARLY YEARS

Jimmy Page held a unique position among the young British guitarists who emerged to change the course of pop music in the sixties. Not for Jimmy overnight success in a chart topping beat group nor the dose of teenage hysteria, which his contemporaries Jeff Beck and Eric Clapton experienced, however briefly, (despite their acne and ethics, there was a place even for them in the fan mags of the day). There was something odd about Jimmy's route to fame and glory. His whole approach to the music business was more subtle. Softly spoken and artistically inclined, he was also stubborn, secretive and determined to do things his own way. He made liaisons, worked behind the scenes, and built up his reputation where it counted. People encouraged him and wanted him under their wing, but he was always anxious to learn enough to take the reins. If his early years appear somewhat of a muddle, without any clear direction, he was actually hacking a path through the jungle of the music business heading for hidden treasure. He rarely made mistakes, even if he seemed to be taking a tortuous route.

Clapton and Beck flirted with fame quite early on, in the Yardbirds, and in Eric's case with John Mayall and then Cream. For some years Page remained an underground cult figure. Yet Jimmy was closer to the hub of the swinging sixties' pop scene than any of them. A combination of health considerations and chance meetings meant that Jimmy spent his early years in the studios, rather than slogging endlessly around the country on one night stands. He earned more and learned more lending his authoritative electric guitar sound to a vast number of record dates. Throughout most of the decade he was hard at work filling out the sound of 'one hit wonder' groups, backing ballad singers anxious to sound up-to-date, and covering up for studio time-wasters.

The work, however, wasn't without its creative rewards and opportunities; his ringing introduction to Joe Cocker's 'With A Little Help From My Friends' was a fanfare for the day when he would lead his own group and emerge from the shadows. In the meantime he got to know a vast number of influential people, from Dusty Springfield to Jackie DeShannon (with whom he had a 'whirlwind romance'), and great svengali manager figures of the period like Andrew Loog Oldham of the Rolling Stones, and Giorgio Gomelsky, Mickie Most, Simon Napier-Bell and Peter Grant all who had a hand in the affairs of The Yardbirds. In such company Jimmy couldn't help but learn there was more to the music business than just a schoolboyish infatuation with rock'n'roll.

● *A smart young Mod circa 1964. Jimmy Page (right) with Viv Prince (left).*

He was born James Patrick Page on January 9, 1944 in Heston, Middlesex, a child of the post-war rock'n'roll boom. He grew up listening to the music of Elvis Presley, Bill Haley, Little Richard and Gene Vincent, but there were no early signs that he would one day become a rock idol in his own right. His father, James Page, was an industrial personnel manager and his mother Elizabeth, worked as a doctor's secretary. The first part of Jimmy's childhood was spent living at the large country house which belonged to his uncle playing in some 400 acres of grounds, fishing and collecting stamps. No stranger to the contents of stately homes he later developed an appreciation of antiques and objets d'art.

When he was eight the family had to move to Feltham, a West London suburb uncomfortably close to London Airport. At school he was said to be 'a bit of a loner' and most of his spare time was spent listening to records or the radio although he sang in the school choir and even became a hurdles champion. A guitar first appeared in the Page household when Jimmy was twelve years old; a Spanish style guitar with steel strings given to his parents by family friends and passed on to Jimmy. It lay around the house untouched for several years until Jimmy was

● *Straight out of the box. Jimmy tunes up backstage at Manchester University.*

turned on by the new teenage passion for rock'n'roll. He picked up the guitar to pose like his new heroes, and gradually learnt how to coax forth notes and even chords.

As the noise of jet aircraft at Heathrow airport became worse, the family moved to Epsom, where Jimmy attended the grammar school, where he made friends with fellow record collectors, rock fans and would-be guitarists. He remembers going onto the playing field one day and seeing another boy surrounded by a crowd of admirers, singing a skiffle song and playing the guitar. 'I wondered how he did it', says Jimmy. 'He showed me how to tune it and it went on from there, going to guitar shops, hanging around watching what other people were doing, until in the end, it was going the other way, and people were watching me.'

Although Jimmy got the famous guitar tutor book *Play In a Day* by Bert Weedon, he found musical theory difficult to master and in any case, the tunes in the books were dull and old fashioned. What he really wanted was to be able to recreate the exciting guitar solos he heard on his favourite records, in particular Elvis Presley's 'Baby Let's Play House.' He loved the guitar work of Scotty Moore, (featured on many other Elvis hits) and James Burton with Ricky Nelson was another of his guitar favourites. He also developed an early appreciation for the work of folk players using acoustic guitars, like Bert Jansch who he described as 'a real dream weaver and incredibly original.' Says Jimmy: 'I wanted to know what it was all about. My friend at school showed me a few chords and I just went on from there. The records generated so much energy I had to be a part of it. That's when I started.'

Another close friend during this period was Jeff Beck who Jimmy met through Jeff's sister. 'He came round to my house with a home-made guitar and played the James Burton solo from Ricky Nelson's 'My Babe' and we were immediately like blood brothers, and we're still friends of course.' Slowly Jimmy began to master the guitar sufficiently and to match his friend's prowess, without any formal lessons. 'I just picked it up. When I was at school I had my guitar confiscated every day. They handed it back to me each afternoon at four o'clock. When I first realised that rock'n'roll was not just Guy Mitchell and Pat Boone, but that something was really going on in there, I knew it was for me.'

Jimmy left school at the age of fifteen intent on making a living as a guitarist. The nearest he came to taking a regular job was when he had an interview, while still at school, for a post as a laboratory assistant. Instead he took a job as lead guitarist with top local band Neil Christian and the Crusaders. As soon as Jimmy had mastered a few chords he felt the need to play with other musicians. 'I used to play in many groups . . . anyone who could get a gig together,' he says. 'It was Neil Christian who saw me playing in a local hall and suggested I play in his band.' To equip himself with guitars he had taken on a paper round. First he got a Grazioso and fitted it with an electric pick-up. He kept this for about eighteen months before getting an orange Gretsch Country Gentleman. Jeff Beck went to see him play with Neil Christian and commented later: 'The guitar looked huge on him because he was such a shrimp. All you saw was a huge guitar being thrown around by a man who was as thin as a pipe cleaner.'

Beck, Page and another local guitarist, Eric Clapton, formed something of a mutual admiration society as they all played around the Epsom and Richmond area at such legendary gigs as the Eel Pie Island hotel, on an island in the Thames. Jimmy played frequently at a dance hall in Epsom with a local band and one night they were booked to support the Dave Clark Five. Neil Christian, then managing a Gene Vincent style group called Red Lewis and The Red Caps, was in the audience. Says Jimmy: 'We started to chat and he asked whether I'd like to play in London, which of course I did. He had to talk to my parents first which was quite a courteous thing to do. I was tailored in the mould to do what all young lads

do, which was to go through school and pass exams. Certainly being a rock'n'roll musician wasn't the choicest of professions, but he reassured my parents and said he'd keep a watchful eye on this young lad, and anyway the gigs were at weekends.'

Neil wanted Jimmy to play with his own group the Crusaders who were making quite a name for themselves. They played a lot of Rock and Blues material and songs by Chuck Berry and Bo Diddley. Other musicians were immediately impressed when they saw the young Page at work with the Crusaders. The young pop fans who went to the gigs were probably more concerned with hearing cover versions of the latest chart hits than noticing what the lead guitar player was laying down. But among those who appreciated his talent was a keyboard player from Sidcup, John Baldwin, who became John Paul Jones in Led Zeppelin seven or so years later. Says John: 'I rated Jimmy Page for years and years. Even in 1962 I can remember people saying "You've got to go and listen to Neil Christian and the Crusaders. They've got this unbelievable young guitarist." I had heard of Pagey before I heard of Clapton or Beck.'

'My friend at school showed me a few chords and I just went on from there'
JIMMY PAGE

Jimmy was getting his first taste of touring. He travelled up to the West End clutching his guitar case and feeling like a hardened pro. He was already earning £20 a week when the average lab assistant would be lucky to get £10. Jimmy spent most of his money on guitars. Neil Christian was delighted with his discovery. 'I took on Jimmy Page when he was still at school' he recalled. 'I talked to his parents because they wanted him to stay on at school and not leave for some rock'n'roll band, but I talked them into it. He played with the Crusaders for several months before deciding he wanted to do session playing. On leaving he suggested Jeff Beck as his replacement, but I didn't take him on.'

Apart from playing with the Crusaders on the road, Jimmy also became involved in fringe activities, and was once spotted providing musical accompaniment for 'beat poet' Royston Ellis at the Mermaid Theatre. Rock writer and broadcaster John Tobler recalls seeing Jimmy: 'Sitting on a bar stool playing nice little guitar fills while Royston recited his "Jiving With Gyp" poems.'

The gruelling life of an itinerant musician soon began to take its toll. The endless round of one night stands affected his health. He suffered from travel sickness and caught glandular fever. Says Jimmy: 'We were driving around the country, sleeping in the van and breaking down on the M1. Eventually it knocks you out. I just collapsed from exhaustion. After only a few months with the band I wondered if I could carry on much longer. I was doing a lot of painting in my free time and thought I would go to art college where a lot of my friends had gone.' And so Jimmy left Neil Christian, without recording with the Crusaders. When Neil went to make his records for EMI the prevailing system demanded that session men were called in as the backing groups of the day weren't considered good enough to be allowed into a studio (the Beatles would change all that within a couple of years).

Although Jimmy was planning on becoming an art student, the music scene wasn't going to let him go too easily. Just as he handed in his notice to Neil, the harmonica player Cyril Davies, who had just broken away from Alexis Korner's Blues Incorporated, asked Jimmy to join his new band. 'I thought it would be awful to go with him and really start enjoying it and then getting ill again, but I did in fact play with them for a bit.' Jimmy was worried that Neil Christian might think he was being disloyal and was quitting in favour of Cyril Davies. But Jimmy felt he could jam by night at the Marquee in Soho, and lead the life of a student by day, without getting sick again. 'I went to art college at Sutton, although I was also accepted by Croydon,' recalls Jimmy, 'I don't know how because I was a terrible draughtsman.'

He was now seventeen years old and felt the music scene was in a bad way. 'When I first started at art college the scene was pretty depressing. All people wanted was Top Twenty stuff and Trad jazz. Then about a year later everything started to happen. The Stones broke through and there were the Liverpool and down south Rhythm and Blues scenes coming together. I enjoyed playing again and Rhythm and Blues restored my faith in pop music. I really wanted to be a fine art painter. I was sincere in that aim and when I went to college I kept quiet that I played guitar or else they would expect me to play in the lunch hour. A conflict arose between music and art and it came to the point where I had to make a decision. I had to leave college because I couldn't do both.'

Cyril Davies was one of the key figures of the emerging British Rhythm and Blues scene. He had started out as a trad jazz banjo player and later helped Alexis form Blues Incorporated which had introduced the concept of electrified Chicago styled Rhythm and Blues to England with all that meant for the future development of rock music. Cyril had left Alexis to concentrate more on the Muddy Waters style of fast rolling blues with his own group. Among those who played alongside him were Jimmy, Nicky Hopkins on piano and singer Long John Baldry. Jamming with Cyril was invaluable experience for Jimmy and it gave him the first taste of blues freedom away from the constraints of a touring pop band. He could also polish up his blues licks in the company of Jeff Beck and Eric Clapton, practising in his parents' front room, especially given over to the guitar obsessed teenagers. There were no rehearsals with Cyril Davies. They just played in the interval at the Marquee between sets by the star attraction. One night they played opposite Muddy Waters; in Britain with a blues package, and armed with a guitar player called Matthew Murphy, who turned out to have played on many of Jimmy's favourite Chuck Berry records.

It was through his appearances at the Marquee that Jimmy came to the attention of producer Mike Leander who was looking for a guitarist to play on a session for a band called Carter-Lewis & The Southerners, the leaders of which, a few years later became better known as The Ivy League. In fact Jimmy had his first taste of session work some time earlier, but with less than happy results. He had been invited to play on the session which produced 'Diamonds' a 1963 hit by ex-Shadows Jet Harris and Tony Meehan, who had formed a highly successful duo. His friend Glyn Johns, who became one of British rock's foremost engineers and producers, had introduced Jimmy to the session, which proved a chastening affair, as Page recalls. 'What went wrong was they stuck a row of dots in front of me, which looked like crows on telegraph wires, which was awful. I could have played it so easily, and it was so simple when another chap came and did it – I realised what had to be done. I'd never bothered or tried to read music. So they said I'd better play the acoustic bit, and when the other chap played this simple sort of riff I gave myself hell for it. It wasn't so much a matter of a lost opportunity as a matter of pride – I felt really stupid.' Things went much better when he was asked to play on the Carter-Lewis session which resulted in 'Your Mama's Out Of Town' which got into the charts. And so his first two sessions had resulted in hits. 'That gave me the impetus to keep on doing it.'

Countless sessions followed where Jimmy was the producer's insurance policy to avoid time wasting in the studio and to strengthen weak links among the players. The Beatles and Stones had crashed on the scene and everyone was desperate for the big beat guitar sound. Jimmy was in the right place at the right time. There were only two other young session guitarists who could cope, Big Jim Sullivan and Vic Flick. Jimmy worked a lot on Decca sessions, although not all of them were hits, and if they were, it wasn't just because of his guitar playing. Between 1963 and 1966 he played on hundreds of record dates, many with top bands who couldn't always get it together in the studio. Egos and temperaments clashed, but Jimmy kept his head down, while taking a crash course in reading 'the dots' and chords. He was no longer embarrassed by the job in hand, although there were still a few difficult moments.

The worst came when he recorded Them, from

● *A split nail or a moment of truth.*

Northern Ireland, fronted by Van Morrison. They had a team of session players on hand virtually duplicating the group; 'You can imagine the tension and what these chaps from Ulster must have thought', says Jimmy. 'It was so embarrassing that you just had to look at the floor and play because they were glaring. It could have been the end of their musical career in one evening. As each number passed, another member of the band would be substituted for by a session musician. It was really horrifying. Talk about daggers! God, It was awful.' There were many times when Jimmy wished the earth would swallow him up, when top groups came into record and found their producers had lined up other people to play on their records. Jimmy played on Them's hits 'Baby Please

• *Relaxing before the gig. January 1971.*

Don't Go', 'Gloria' and 'Here Comes The Night.' He also experienced tension when he was called in by producer Shel Talmy to help the Kinks on *You Really Got Me* album. The Kinks didn't want him around, understandably they felt Dave Davies could do the job perfectly well. Usually cost conscious producers wanted things done well, but quickly. In fact Dave Davies was the guitarist on the Kinks' classic 'You Really Got Me' and Jimmy ended up playing the tambourine, according to Ray Davies.

Jimmy played with a host of sixties' pop names including Donovan, Mickie Most, Chris Farlowe, Lulu, P.J. Proby, Cliff Richard, Brenda Lee, The Rolling Stones, Burt Bacharach, Val Doonican, The Bachelors, and The Who. He played on the latter's 'I Can't Explain' to fill out the guitar sound.

He met all manner of artists during his first eighteen highly successful months in the studio and formed a songwriting partnership with singer Jackie DeShannon who paid his fare to make a flying visit to America. He started to get royalty cheques for songs he'd writted for Marianne Faithfull, P.J. Proby and Esther Phillips. Perhaps they saw him as a pleasant, affable, and talented key figure to the underworld of rock, normally inhabited by uncommunicative, neanderthal beings. Jimmy was hip, reliable and soon to become highly fashionable – much to his alarm he

was even featured in a Sunday colour supplement article. Even so he tried to play down his role as the behind-the-scenes man on other people's rcords. He knew it might breed resentment and damage his own prospects when he eventually branched out on his own.

Years later many of his best records from the period were collected onto a bootleg album called *James Patrick Page Session Man* issued in 1979 by a dubious body called the Led Zeppelin Fan Club of Manchester. The songs showed how Jimmy's guitar style had developed, with its use of fuzz and distortion and there's no doubt he made great strides from his hesitant strumming on 'Diamonds' to the driving lead played on Dave Berry's version of Chuck Berry's

'I really wanted to be a fine art painter'
JIMMY PAGE

'Memphis Tennessee.' The album also revealed such long forgotten items as 'Talking About You' by The Redcaps, (presumably the group that Neil Christian managed) which was originally released on Decca in 1963. Sometimes he tried to play faster than his technique allowed but one of his best early solos was on 'My Baby Left Me' – the B side of 'Memphis Tennessee.'

Jimmy and the 'hidden brotherhood' of older session men gradually got used to each other, although, sometimes when Jimmy let fly with some blazing guitar work the brass players would tend to stick their fingers in their ears in pointed fashion. And Jimmy never quite got the hang of all those sheets of music. He recalls: 'For the first eighteen months it was really enjoyable, and I'd come to terms with the technical side and having to read music. Although I could never read music in the same way that I could read a newspaper, I could scan through a sheet of music and know it by the time they counted the song in. So I never actually learned to read although I wish I had.' After a while the novelty of endless sessions with artists he didn't know or care about began to wear off. He explains: 'Everyone likes to play around with different people and it can be stimulating to do sessions with other groups. But the kind of work I was doing became completely stifling. Never being involved with the artist it was like being a computer. Work escalated. But there was no individuality involved. The arranger said: "This is what you play," and that's what I played. I got fed up. It became a pain in the neck.' Sometimes 'fixers' booked him for sessions that turned out to be recording 'Muzak' for supermarkets. One of his weirdest assignments was to play on an album by Irish vocal group The Bachelors, called *Bachelors' Girls* and released in 1966 on which he played one of the worst solos of his career on a song called 'Lovey Kravezit' – out of tune and tongue-in-cheek.

More to Jimmy's taste was a session for his drummer friend Bobbie Graham, who recorded a version of Louis Bellson's 'Skin Deep' drum solo. Jimmy co-wrote the B-side 'Zoom, Widge And Wag' and played on both sides. This was the closest Jimmy had come to recording heavy rock, as opposed to the fast, jerky rock'n'roll of the Beat Boom era. The production gave unusual prominence to the drums with lots of echo and some background screaming.

Eventually he cut his own single called 'She Just Satisfies' coupled with 'Keep Movin' which was released on Fontana in 1965. Jimmy later claimed that he 'did it for fun' and that he played all the instruments except the drums, which were played by Bobbie Graham. 'I sang on it too which is quite unique' said Jimmy. 'When I got to the studio I didn't know what the hell I was gonna do. The A-side was tongue-in-cheeks Kinks. Jackie DeShannon helped me salvage the whole thing. The end product I suppose was a trip to the States to see her. But the record is best forgotten.'

Jimmy also worked with Mickie Most, now head of RAK records. In the early sixties Mickie was still aiming for success as a singer and Jimmy played on such Most singles as 'The Feminine Look', 'Money Honey' and 'That's Alright.' He also worked with The Everly Brothers when they cut the LP *Two Yanks In England* and produced 'Hang On Sloopy' by The McCoy's for Immediate Records, Andrew Oldham's Independent label. Becoming house producer and arranger for Immediate he worked on albums for the vocal duo, Twice As Much, and for one of his favourite singers, Chris Farlowe. He also produced sessions for Nico, Fleur De Lys and John Mayall and the Bluesbreakers. It was one of his first jobs to produce the single 'I'm Not Saying' by the German singer Nico, who would later achieve fame in Velvet Underground. The John Mayall sessions resulted in the single 'I'm Your Witchdoctor' and 'Telephone Blues.' They also cut 'Sitting On Top Of The World' and 'Double Crossing Time'.

Jimmy first bumped into Eric Clapton in a recording studio lobby when Eric was on his way out and Jimmy was just arriving. 'They tell me you play a bit of Matt Murphy' said Eric. 'Well I have a shot,' said Jimmy. Later Jimmy and Jeff Beck went to see Eric playing a gig with the Bluesbreakers. Eric came to stay at Page's home that night and in the morning started jamming on some handy guitars. A cheap two channel tape recorder was left running. When Jimmy later produced the 'Telephone Blues' session he mentioned to Immediate executives the existence of the Clapton-Page jam tapes. They immediately claimed them for release, insisting that the artists were under contract. It was a shoddy trick, and Jimmy was unhappy about the idea of Eric being exploited. When he realised he couldn't prevent the company taking the tapes and putting them out on the *Blues Anytime* albums, he insisted that at least the tracks be improved with Mick Jagger playing harmonica and the Stones' rhythm section supplying a cohesive beat.

Eric was promised some royalties. Says Jimmy: 'Eric and I got split writing on the tunes, but I don't remember getting any money out of it. I don't know if

● *Jimmy plays acoustic at Roy Harper gig, 1974.*

Eric did. It was a bit of a drag that it should ever have come out. I just had no power at all to stop them. It was just an experiment, and it wasn't done in the way in which it finally appeared. I think everybody was cheated at the end of the day on that.' Immediate Records folded not long after the release of the albums in question, although they have been issued under titles, including *Anthology of British Blues* and *Blues Anytime*. The Page and Clapton cuts were about the best things on them.

It was all invaluable experience in learning about the pitfalls of the music business, not to mention the best way to achieve success in the studio. Jimmy could also see the changes coming, as the guitar sound fell out of favour with producers who began to use Stax style riffing horns or even full orchestras. Nevertheless Jimmy would still be on hand to supply the hot licks, sometimes in the most surprising company. 'I'd do a session with jazz saxophonist Tubby Hayes, then sometimes with Petula Clark, and to follow that anything from rock'n'roll to a jingle to a folk session I was really having to stretch my musical resources and knowledge without even realising it, which was really good as far as discipline and education went,' Jimmy told John Tobler in an interview. Jimmy even played harmonica on some sessions for Cliff Richard, David Bowie and Mickey Finn & The Blue Men. It was back to guitar though for Tom Jones' smash hit 'It's Not Unusual' and for more sessions with Georgie Fame, Herman's Hermits, and Crispian St Peters.

Jimmy eventually formed his own publishing company called James Page Music and among the groups who recorded songs he published were The Quik, The Majority and The Outsiders. One of his major production efforts was 'The Bells Of Rhymney' by Fifth Avenue, which he wrote and arranged, using John Paul Jones on bass guitar. Jimmy was not content to stick to the rules and conventions of the sixties' studio scene. 'I remember when I did the sessions with Eric Clapton for Immediate,' recalls Jimmy. 'I was producing and Eric started using feedback on one number. The engineer who'd never heard it before screamed out "This is totally unrecordable!". So we put the faders up. They were good sessions.' He began to experiment with using a violin bow on his guitar strings. Later this became one of Jimmy's most celebrated trademarks. 'But that wasn't actually my idea,' he says. 'It was suggested to me by one of the violinists in the string section.' He denied it was just a gimmick but felt that it produced a valid musical sound. 'It sounds like an orchestra at times, it's quite amazing! The only drawback to the technique is that a guitar has a flat neck as opposed to a violin's curved neck, which is a bit limiting.'

In 1965 a chance came for Jimmy to quit the studios and return to the road. He was offered the job of replacing Eric Clapton, who had quit The Yardbirds in protest at the increasingly commercial policy, and joined John Mayall's Bluesbreakers. Jimmy turned down the offer as he didn't like the way it was put to him by the garrulous Gomelsky and he wasn't ready to leave the comfort of the studios and risk another bout of touring. Jeff Beck who was then with The Tridents, took the job instead. He later invited Jimmy to join him in The Yardbirds but for the meantime Jimmy hung on to his job at Immediate. He backed Chris Farlowe on his big hit 'Out Of Time' and helped Mick Jagger and Andrew Oldham make demos.

Jimmy just couldn't go on restricting his guitar playing to a few bar breaks on the B-sides of other people's hits. He would have to start stretching out and playing in public again. It would mean less money and increased strain on his health, but Jimmy knew he had to go. Says Jimmy: 'It was fate.'

CHAPTER THREE
'TRAIN KEPT A ROLLIN'

The Yardbirds were young, bright and articulate. They managed to be both convincing purveyors of home-brewed rhythm and blues and successful pop artists. This should have made them happy, but they were often racked with dissent and inner conflict.

Born out of the R&B boom engendered by the Rolling Stones, the 'most blueswailing' Yardbirds became known as a breeding ground for guitar talent. They employed four lead players during the various stages of their career, three of whom became among the most influential in rock. Their original guitarist Anthony 'Top' Topham was only fifteen years old when the band started out as the Metropolis Blues Quartet in sunny suburban Richmond during the early sixties. Older and more experienced player Eric Clapton was brought into replace Topham in 1963 and during his stay with the band, up until 1965, they moved up from supporting the Stones at the Crawdaddy Club to headlining status. When Eric left he was replaced by Jeff Beck, who was later joined by Jimmy Page in 1966. Before Page arrived on the scene The Yardbirds had already enjoyed their finest hours. They had an assured reputation for recreating on-stage excitement and imaginative hit records like 'For Your Love' 'Heartful Of Soul' and 'Still I'm Sad'.

The core of the band consisted of Keith Relf (vocals and harmonica), Paul Samwell-Smith (bass), Chris Dreja (rhythm guitar) and Jim McCarty (drums). They had a love hate relationship with their star guitarists, always seeking the best, but never quite knowing how to utilise such great talent. They were one of the first bands to allow their guitarist to go completely berserk in a 'rave up' on blues standards like 'Smokestack Lightning', which were turned into vehicles for wild improvisation, feedback and all the volume their speakers could take. While The Rolling Stones stuck pretty much to conventional Chess Records style rhythm and blues, the Yardbirds were all for experimenting. They were ahead of The Who and The Kinks in creating uproar, in fact most experts on heavy metal say the genre started with The Yardbirds. In their smart Mod clothes and Brian Jones fringes, The Yardbirds were always setting trends.

As often happens to pioneers they failed to consolidate their success and towards the end of their career became lost, frustrated, dazed and confused. The first major blow came when Eric Clapton quit to join John Mayall's Blues Breakers, just when The Yardbirds had their first major hit with 'For Your Love'.

Eric was a star, already hailed by his fans as 'God'. Finding a replacement would be difficult. Giorgio Gomelsky told Jimmy Page that Eric was 'taking a holiday' and asked if he would join. Jimmy didn't want to usurp Clapton's role so he told the band he didn't feel fit enough to travel and wanted to carry on with session work. He recommended they use his friend Jeff Beck, then playing at Eel Pie Island with The Tridents.

The group were moving on from their staple diet of blues tunes and trying out Gregorian chants and Indian music. Jeff, with his skill at sustaining notes and creating weird sounds proved an ideal replacement. He had been using feedback, by pushing his guitar up against the speakers and causing them to howl, for several years before joining the group. His prowess was particularly well displayed on the band's first studio album *The Yardbirds* released in July 1966 and now known as *Roger The Engineer* from its cover drawing by Chris Dreja of Roger Cameron of Advision Studios.

Jeff proved difficult to get on with. As a mixed-up, tongue-tied youth, who found touring a terrible strain,

● *Interview album featuring Jim McCarty and Chris Dreja recorded in February 1982. The rare cover shot shows Page and Beck (Foreground). Courtesy Rhino Records. (Taken from Rhino LP RNDF 253).*

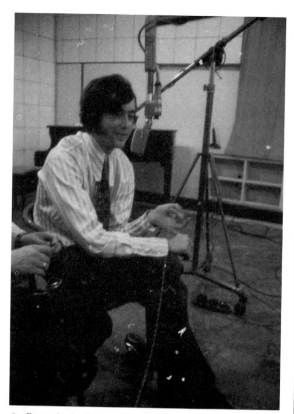

● *Jimmy in the throes of '60s session work – dig the shirt!*

Ball at Oxford University. Keith Relf was antagonised by the upper class guests who obviously didn't think much of his or The Yardbirds' performance. There was no reaction, so Keith retaliated by getting drunk, blowing raspberries into the microphone, rolling on the floor and swearing at the tuxedo clad guests. Keith had to be pulled off and the band played instrumentals for the rest of the set. Paul Samwell-Smith, ex-Grammar school and potential stockbroker, was most upset and embarrassed by this display. He'd already grown restless with the riotous life on the road, and decided he wanted to leave and concentrate on becoming a producer.

Watching events that night with considerable amusement was Jimmy Page. He recalled later: 'They were a good band to go and see. Then came this great night at Oxford. Keith Relf was incredibly pissed, rolling around the stage, blowing his harmonica in all the wrong places and making up nonsense lyrics. Eventually he just collapsed into the drum kit. It was great. But instead of seeing the humour of it, the bass player Paul Samwell-Smith just blew up and said "I can't stand this anymore. I'm going to leave the group, and if I were you Keith I'd do the same

'We did a tour with the Stones and they got quite worried about us!'
JIM McCARTY

thing."' The group once again asked Jimmy if he would join and this time he accepted. It was supposed to be a temporary measure but it soon became obvious that it was a permanent post with a view to promotion. Although he wasn't playing his proper instrument, Jimmy just enjoyed being in this erratic band which had so much potential. And in August, soon after Jimmy's arrival, the band went off to America. Jimmy had just two hours rehearsal with them at the Marquee.

Out on the road in the States, Jeff Beck became increasingly difficult. He failed to turn up for a gig at the Carousel Club in San Francisco, and Jimmy took over on lead guitar and Chris Dreja played bass. Jimmy felt nervous about playing lead because the band were at the peak of their fame in the States and expectation among the fans was high. But Jimmy proved to be brilliant on lead and from then on there was no question of him returning to obscurity as a bassist. That night, Jimmy Page, lead guitarist, stepped out and became his own man. When Jeff Beck turned up again, he would have to share lead duties with Jimmy. Recalls Jim McCarty: 'Jeff kept letting us down. Chris went on bass and Jimmy

he became increasingly unreliable, and perhaps felt his starring role flattering, but also a burden. He tentatively asked Jimmy Page to come into the band to help him out, but Page still held out. Meanwhile the group were taken over by another manager, Simon Napier-Bell, and the band toured America with considerable success. They were bringing coals to Newcastle, as young white Americans heard their own heritage of blues music for the first time, delivered by attractive kids they could relate to and understand. The Yardbirds inspired dozens of immitators and some support bands in the States actually played the whole of The Yardbirds' set before the English group came on. Steven Tyler of Aerosmith, was one of many stars of later years who credited The Yardbirds for turning them onto music.

The Yardbirds' tour of America may have encouraged Jimmy to change his mind. The group were chosen to play in Antonioni's Swinging Sixties movie *Blow Up* which starred David Hemmings as a fashion photographer who witnesses a murder. One of the key scenes took place in a night club, actually a film set version of the Ricky Tick Club in Windsor, which somehow got transferred in the movie to Oxford Street. Jeff Beck appeared smashing up his guitar in the final moments of 'Train Kept A Rollin'. In the background could be seen the group's new bass player, Jimmy Page.

The events which led to Jimmy playing bass and not lead guitar were set in motion the night of the May played lead. We had a Dick Clark Caravan tour to do which was really hard work, playing two towns a night. Jeff did a couple of nights and really wasn't into it at all. He blew his top and smashed his Les Paul up in the dressing room. So he went back to England and we finished the tour with Jimmy on lead. Originally it was Jeff's idea to bring Jimmy into the group but I think they had a few differences. They would try and outdo each other's solos and it put Jeff under quite a bit of strain. It was exciting but it was bloody loud! They used to do 'Over, Under, Sideways, Down' as a stereo dual guitar riff. I remember we did a tour with the Stones and they got quite worried about us! We finished with Jimmy as our lead guitarist around 1968.'

Jimmy remembers the incident when Jeff exploded in rage. 'I walked into the dressing room and Beck had his guitar up over his head, about to bring it down on Keith Relf's head, but instead smashed in on the floor. Relf looked at him with total astonishment and Beck said: "Why did you make me do that?"'

Beck went off to see his girlfriend in Los Angeles, much more fun than messing around with The Yardbirds for lousy money. He had already shown his displeasure before Jimmy joined The Yardbirds by knocking over amps on stage and turning up late for gigs. He had pulled himself together more on stage when Jimmy joined, out of respect for a fellow player.

● *Yardbirds with Page and Beck (right).*

But his off-stage antics remained just as wild. Understandably the mild-mannered boys from Richmond and Kingston had suffered enough. A meeting was held and Beck was told he couldn't work with them anymore. Jeff expected Jimmy to leave as well, but Page had decided to stay on and see what could be salvaged.

About the only recorded evidence of the period when Jeff and Jimmy shared lead was the two tracks they cut in England 'Happenings Ten Years Time Ago' and 'Psycho Daisies.' The A-side was written by Keith Relf and Jim McCarty, and featured many of the new psychedelic influences then creeping into rock music from the West Coast. There was a 'bomb' explosion and police siren noises from Jeff's guitar, and the whole piece was a sardonic commentary on life in a rock group. Unfortunately the record wasn't a hit. It was considered too far out. Indeed few even among the musicians can remember who played what on the record. Some thought John Paul Jones sat in on bass while Jimmy played second lead. Their only other recording in this period was the one number they played on the soundtrack of *Blow Up*, which was Johnny Burnette's 'Train Kept A Rollin' retitled 'Stroll On' for copyright reasons.

Back in England The Yardbirds toured with Ike and Tina Turner and the Rolling Stones, which had been the only chance British fans got to see them with the twin guitar line up before their final bust up with Jeff in America. Simon Napier-Bell was replaced by a new manager, Peter Grant, who took the band to Singapore and Australia and for the first time in their

● *Page rubs barnets with Andy Warhol but is this party shot a faked cut out?*

career the band actually began to see some real money coming their way. But their record company were unhappy at the lack of success in the singles market, and Mickie Most, a friend and partner of Peter Grant's was brought in to produce some singles. The first was called 'Little Games' which was the title of their album released on Epic and only in America at the time. Other tracks cut during this 1967 period included 'Ha Ha Said The Clown' and 'Ten Little Indians'.

The band didn't really like handing over creative control and felt if they had been left to their own devices with Jimmy Page up front, they could soon have recovered all their old vitality and spirit and produced something exciting of their own. With the exception of Jimmy, they were feeling weary and bruised after years on the road. Also Jim McCarthy and Keith Relf were being increasingly influenced by psychedelia and flower power not to mention LSD. They began sporting kaftans, beads and bells and burning incense in their hotel bedrooms. They began to take gigs less seriously and on one occasion Jim failed to turn up at the airport for a trip to America and an American drummer filled in until Jim had recovered from his breakdown.

On the stage The Yardbirds were still a force to be reckoned with and among the tunes they performed were 'Waiting For The Man' borrowed from The Velvet Underground and a new song called 'Dazed And Confused'. Unfortunately their support at home was in irreversible decline and morale was not helped by bad reviews. Jimmy told me: 'When we went over to the States we took them by storm. The funny thing was The Yardbirds didn't mean anything as a group in England. There was no magic attached to the name. In America it was different. Hollywood went wild. Anyway – it was an exciting group. But when we played at the Royal Albert Hall in London the English papers said "The Yardbirds appeared with their cacophony of sound." Of course in those days groups used the Albert Hall PA system and you know what that's like. The guitars were really loud – and bad! Eric had always used a little amp and that was Keith Relf's big complaint about Jeff and me. Keith would say "Eric used to play through an AC30

and you've got 300 watts each!'' He got more and more reticent, but nobody was trying to drown him out. Obviously there was a lot of tension, and that's why he made two solo records.' Chris Dreja recalled those hectic days: 'When it worked, it was incredible, all those stereo rifs and alternating voices, but it frequently degenerated into a wall of noise.'

With Jeff gone the band tightened up; Jimmy was featured on a number called 'White Summer' and used the violin bow on 'Tinker, Tailor, Soldier, Sailor'. Peter Grant took them on tours of Germany, Sweden, France and Belgium but while Jimmy could see potential for hard electric rock with lots of lead guitar work, the rest of the band were leaning towards flower power and lyrical songs. Early in 1968 Keith and Jim announced that they wanted to leave the band. They were booked for one last tour of America playing ballrooms and universities. The worst gig on the tour as far as the band were concerned was The Anderson Theatre in New York, a cold, unfriendly place which they never liked playing. Unfortunately Epic, their American record company had heard the band were about to break up and tried to get one more album out of them by recording them 'Live' at the Anderson Theatre. The same night Vanilla Fudge were playing across town which drew away many of the fans. In addition the engineers Epic sent to record the gig had no idea how to cope with the sound of an electric rock band; there was one microphone for the drum kit, and only a couple of others draped around the stage. The results were predictably poor. Jimmy Page's monitor speaker was 'miked' in mistake for the main speaker, which meant all the fuzz tones and sustained notes went missing. The band were assured that if the recording wasn't up to scratch it would be put on file and not released. Later they heard the results and found that the head of the light music department who had been assigned to the job, had overdubbed the sounds of cheers (allegedly taken from a recording of a bullfight), in a desperate attempt to introduce some atmosphere. Jimmy Page listened in disbelief to the results: 'There were all these bullfight cheers dubbed on it every time there was a solo and it was just awful. You'd play a solo then this huge "Rah" would come leaping out at you. There was one number where there was supposed to be utter silence in the audience and this guy dubbed in the clinking of glasses and a whole night club atmoshere.' Despite the band's insistence that the tapes be put on the shelf, Epic released *'Live Yardbirds With Jimmy Page At The Anderson Theatre'* in 1971 when Led Zeppelin were at their peak. Jimmy had an injunction put on the company and the record was swiftly withdrawn. Columbia Special Projects re-issued it again with the original cover and tracks in 1975.

In fact the band played well that night. The record has been available on bootleg tapes ever since and gives a valuable insight into how the band's music was developing. Several riffs and ideas then in use would turn up later on Led Zeppelin's first album, albeit improved beyond The Yardbirds' wildest dreams.

Jimmy was anxious to forge ahead. Now that he had acquired the taste for being back on the road and up front in a top band with lots of freedom to play, he was ready for more. Sadly Keith and Jim couldn't go on. Since leaving school The Yardbirds had been their life. Now they wanted to go off and do something entirely new. Jimmy explained that with all his session experience, it would be perfectly feasible for the band to change around and try new things within their existing format. He was sorry to see the band break up without making a proper album with him. 'I tried desperately to keep them together. The gigs were there, but Keith in particular would not take them very seriously, getting drunk and singing in the wrong places,' lamented Jimmy. By the end the band even seemed ashamed of the name 'Yardbirds' it was associated with the past, pre-psychedelic era.

Jimmy found it hard to understand this attitude. 'I thought they were a great band I was never ashamed of playing in The Yardbirds.' He thought they could have carried on and become one of the greatest groups of all time. But he would have to prove his theories about the appeal of power rock in another band.

While Page had been trying to salvage The Yardbirds during the previous year, Jeff Beck had gone off to form his own band with Rod Stewart as the lead singer. They played at the Finsbury Park Astoria in March 1967 on a package show with The Small

● *Jimmy back in action, with double-neck guitar, at Knebworth, 1979.*

Faces and Roy Orbison. It was not an auspicious start. Rod's zip fly kept coming down causing shrieks of laughter from the girls, and the band forgot their arrangements. Jeff stormed off-stage in a rage.

Later the Jeff Beck Group began to score success in America. Jimmy kept a close eye on their progress. Jimmy and Jeff had played together on a Mickie Most session which produced 'Beck's Bolero', the B-side to Jeff's big hit single, 'Hi Ho Silver Lining', on which Jeff turned singer, while Jeff was also managed by Peter Grant. For the recording of the 'Beck's Bolero' session, Mickie Most brought together an all-star cast; Beck and Page were on guitars, Nicky Hopkins (piano), John Paul Jones (bass), and Keith Moon (drums). Jimmy got the idea then of forming a 'super group' with most of this line up. Keith Moon had suggested bringing in his friend John Entwistle as lead singer and bassist, as both men were undergoing a spell of disenchantment with The Who at the time. After much discussion it was decided to bring in Steve Winwood as singer, but he was tied up with Traffic. Next, they tried Steve Marriott who seemed very enthusiastic about the idea. His management, however, thought otherwise and a message came through to Jimmy along the lines of 'How would you like to play guitar with broken fingers? You will be if you don't stay away from Stevie.' The idea was, not surprisingly, dropped after this incident and The Yardbirds began another tour

---

'How would you like to play a guitar with broken fingers?'

---

which meant Jimmy had to go back to work and stop dreaming. Ironically, the name for this stillborn band was Led Zeppelin. Keith Moon joked that the band would probably go down like a lead balloon. John Entwistle agreed, but felt the disaster would be on an even bigger scale 'like a Led Zeppelin.'

At the beginning of 1968 it seemed like the death knell for the Yardbirds when their equipment was stolen from their van including all of Jimmy's special effects as well as the band's drum kit, amplifiers and PA system. The last American tour began on March 22, 1968 and they played until April 28. They also recorded a *Top Gear* programme for BBC Radio where they played 'Dazed And Confused' (which had started out life as 'I'm Confused' with different lyrics by Keith Relf). Other numbers on the broadcast included 'Think About It', 'White Summer' and 'Goodnight Sweet Josephine'. The band's last public performance was at Luton Technical College in July 1968.

As they went their separate ways, Jimmy began to revive plans for his own group. He would be aided and abetted by Peter Grant. They had become friends during the endless tours of America; Jimmy admired Peter's attitude and ability to get things done, and Peter thought highly of Jim's professionalism and musicianship. He had handled so many temperamental artists that working with a polite gentleman like Jimmy would be a relief and very rewarding. All they needed now was a band, and some work. As it happened, The Yardbirds had left a string of contracted dates unplayed, so work was no problem. Jimmy had not let his old session contacts slip and was working with Donovan in the studio, on the latter's 'Hurdy Gurdy Man', when he met up once again with John Paul Jones who was the arranger on the session. During a break in recording, John asked Jimmy if he could use a bass player in his new group. The band was to be called The New Yardbirds, simply to placate those promoters who were expecting the old ones. Chris Dreja had considered joining the band and even went along to rehearsals, but in the end he decided to quit the music business and became a professional photographer.

Of the remaining Yardbirds, Keith and Jim went off to form Renaissance, which lasted for a couple of years and included Keith's sister Jane, Louis Cennamo and John Hawken, ex-Nashville Teens. They recorded an album for Island in 1970. Sadly Keith Relf died in tragic circumstances a few years later. He was electrocuted by his own guitar while practising at home in 1976. He had just been planning to put a new band together with his old friend Jim McCarty.

In 1983 there was a Yardbirds reunion gig at the Marquee Club featuring Jim McCarty, Paul Samwell-Smith and Chris Dreja with some guest guitarists. Beck, Clapton and Page were all invited. None of them turned up.

CHAPTER FOUR
THE WILD MAN OF BLUES

The Wild Man Of Blues from the Black Country was what they called Robert Plant in the early days. Long before he achieved fame 'down South' Robert was recognised as a precocious talent among the groups and fans of a thriving Midlands scene. When he was finally discovered by Jimmy Page and Peter Grant in time for the creation of Led Zeppelin, Robert already had several years hard singing and recording experience. But with most of the media and the music business centred on London, it was difficult in the mid-sixties to break out and get noticed, unless there was powerful management in the background. That was something that Robert, drifting from group to group, seemed to lack.

Armed with a powerful pair of lungs and great presence, Robert seemed born to the role of fronting a group. Where others seemed shy, awkward and consumed with doubts and personality disorders, Robert exuded confidence. Apart from his commanding physique and good looks, he also had the zeal of an enthusiast, eager to explore and extract full meaning from the blues and the best kinds of pop music. This made his own work seem all the more genuine and authoritative. If he hadn't been a pop singer, Robert, with his intelligence and good education would doubtless have become a successful business or professional man. But as an incurable romantic and adventurer, once he was gripped by rock'n'roll, there was no turning back.

● *The Band Of Joy in London, 1967. Left to right Kevyn Gammond, Paul Lockey, Robert Plant, John Bonham and Chris Brown.*

• *Robert in early Zeppelin mode.*

He was born Robert Anthony Plant on August 20, 1948 in West Bromwich, Staffordshire. He had a sister Allison, born in 1959. His parents were Robert, a civil engineer, and Ann Plant. It was hoped that Robert would become a chartered accountant and he was sent to King Edward VI Grammar school in Stourbridge, Worcestershire. But from an early age he showed signs of interest in music, aroused, as were most kids of his generation by skiffle. When ousting bicycles and stamp collecting were the latest craze, Robert dabbled with home-made instruments such as, the harmonica, kazoo and washboard. It should be explained that in the age before washing machines became universal, housewives had to do their weekly laundry by scrubbing shirts etc. on a wooden board with a serrated metal surface. By placing thimbles on the fingers of each hand and scraping the board, a rhythmic beat could be produced.

Soon skiffle began to pale and listening to Elvis Presley records seemed much more exciting. When Robert went to grammar school he made friends who turned him onto the blues artists who, they felt sure had provided the inspiration for white rock'n'roll. Thus began a fascinating period of exploration in junk shops and record stores seeking out records by Otis Rush, Bukka White, Skip James and Buddy Guy.

After finding the early Sun recordings by Elvis, which were much more 'earthy' than the later pop hits, he also began to listen to singers like Muddy Waters, Howlin' Wolf, Willie Dixon and Sonny Boy Williamson, picking up on their harmonica playing in the process. Robert taught himself to sing with these records, while practising Elvis movements in the bedroom mirror. His growing obsession from the age of thirteen onwards, with music, meant his school work suffered. 'It was decided by my teachers that I was intelligent but unwilling to concentrate,' he recalls. He took an interest in such subjects as archaeology and Roman history, and music lessons were popular, until a Plant style prank, when he hid a pair of gym shoes in the school piano, successfully sabotaging the teacher's attempts to play. Robert was henceforth barred from music lessons. He decided to gain more practical experience in the outside world, and at the age of fifteen, while still at school, began singing in pubs and folk clubs. Underage as far as the licensing laws were concerned, he managed to get a residency at the Seven Stars, a blues club in Old Swinsford. He had started out singing Blind Boy Fuller songs and accompanied himself on the harmonica, kazoo and trusty washboard. The grammar school blues boy must have made a poignant and somewhat baffling sight for pub regulars. As far as Robert was concerned it was all part of his process of self-education. 'As soon as I got the essence of what intrigued me, it was an incessant search, constantly to develop musical taste,' says Robert. 'There was a lot of stuff that you could find, a lot of artists apart from the more recent city bluesmen, the Chicago-Chess Records people. There were the people who came well before Muddy Waters, including Sleepy John Estes, who I really doted on. I especially liked one song, 'Lawyer Clerk Blues' from around 1928.' There were more modern influences too, in particular Ray Clarkes whose 'Drown In My Own Tears' was a favourite. Robert sang Bob Dylan's 'Corrina Corrina' with the Delta Blues Band. Other blues and folk stylists he investigated were Peetie Wheatstraw, Woodie Guthrie and Blind Lemon Jefferson. He was encouraged in his blues discovery course by a friend Terry Foster, from Kidderminster, who played an eight-string guitar and was rumoured to have been involved in The Yardbirds, in their earliest stages.

Naturally Robert also listened to the current beat group scene but was not impressed. He told me: 'I had been surrounded by English rock way back in the early sixties. Some of it was very ballsy, but the majority of it was half-baked, and didn't seem to be

> ## 'You can squeeze my lemon till the juice runs down my leg'
> **ROBERT JOHNSON**

● ABOVE: *In the back of the limo, off to Heathrow, 1971.*

● RIGHT: *Robert on TISWAS (children's ITV show) waiting for a custard pie.*

coming from any place in particular. I'd listen to The Fenmen when they came to the town hall, but I didn't know that 'Money' (a hit for Bern Elliott & The Fenmen), was a Barrett Strong thing. You always heard these things in the context of English rock. Then I'd start to find the originals on the London America label. I started going back to the roots and then I heard Robert Johnson for the first time at the age of fifteen. The influence of Robert Johnson was crucial. Robert, who died at the age of twenty-four back in 1938, was a singer and guitarist who most influenced the Chicago blues school of later years. Many Black American bluesmen came to a violent end, but in Johnson's case he was apparently given a poisoned glass of whiskey in the juke joint he was playing at. It was Johnson who sang the immortal lines 'You can squeeze my lemon till the juice runs down my leg,' later adopted by Robert in Led Zeppelin. Johnson, who lived a harder and more riotous life than most rock stars could imagine, would doubtless have been bemused by the fate of his lyrics and the ramifications of his influence on pop music. His spirit would also be felt in the work of Jimi Hendrix. Says Robert: 'One of the things I picked up from Robert Johnson when I started singing was the liaison between the guitar playing and his voice. It was so sympathetic it almost seemed as if the guitar was his vocal chords. There was a tremendous amount of emotional content in the guitar and the vocals. It was the most amazing thing I'd ever heard. I think Muddy Waters took a lot from his style.'

Robert's own voice began to develop quite early although even he was surprised at his own power and range. 'The voice really started developing when I was fifteen and I was singing Tommy McLean numbers. I don't really know why it is as powerful as it is.' There was growing concern in the Plant household over Robert's preoccupation with blues and pop music. It seemed to be destroying all hopes for a stable future in commerce. But there was no doubt, when he made the effort, and settled down, he could do the work. Robert could even see it from his parents' viewpoint. 'When I was at school I liked all this peculiar music, Chris Kenner's 'I Like It Like That' and all these different kinds of music that weren't akin to a grammar school education . . . where was the boy getting it from? In the end it was agreed in the Plant household that if I did well in my exams, I'd get a copy of 'Help Me' by Sonny Boy Williamson. I came top of the class.'

After a bout of concentrated study, Robert changed out of his school uniform, put on his old blue jeans and set off for the backrooms of the Stourbridge pubs. He had already started to grow his hair long. 'At thirteen-and-a-half I liked girls all of a sudden and it was all down to attracting them the best way I could. I grew my hair. It flopped over my ears and was immediately chopped off.' Girls, football and music have remained Robert's main interests to this day. Although he astounded everyone by getting six GCE 'O' levels and then left school in 1964. To please his father he started work as a trainee accountant, but he only stayed two weeks. 'I can still count faster than an adding machine but I was determined I wasn't going to count other people's money for the rest of my life,' he says. 'I was only being paid £2 a week by the man who was supposed to be teaching me accountancy.' Tension grew at home. Says Robert: 'It was getting to the stage where I only dared to go home at night, because my hair was so long. So at sixteen I left home and started my real education musically . . . moving from group to group, furthering my knowledge of the blues.'

On his travels Robert found that not all English singers were just pale copies of American originals. He heard fifteen year old Stevie Winwood singing with the Spencer Davis Group and was greatly impressed. Robert too was beginning to create an impression. One of his first major local gigs was with Andy Long and The Original Jurymen, when he 'depped' for the lead singer who had laryngitis. Next came work with the Delta Blues Band and the New Memphis Bluesbreakers; these were often very loose outfits with floating personnel. Robert played harmon-

ica with the Delta Blues Band and Mr Plant used to drop Robert off at the Seven Stars. There he would steam into favourites like 'I Got My Mojo Working' jamming alongside Stan Webb, the guitarist who formed Chicken Shack and Chris Wood, who played flute with Traffic. Robert preferred this to the folk clubs where the atmosphere was more serious and intense, with little response to the music beyond the sound of pints being pulled and fresh tobacco being thumbed into pipes. Robert found he needed the applause of a lively audience to make it all worthwhile and meaningful. He played guitar with Black Snake Moan (named after a song by Blind Lemon Jefferson), and later joked: 'It would be terribly hard top guess what the old black snake was.' Next he went to the jazz influenced The Banned and on to The Crawling King Snakes.

By now the music scene was being shaken up by the new Black American pop music – soul as performed by Otis Redding and Wilson Pickett. They were latter day blues men backed up by powerful modern rhythm sections and shouting trumpets and saxes. In the midst of all this excitement, the young and hairy Robert Plant sang his heart out, and the fans began to take notice. It was then he earned the title 'The Wild Man Of Blues From The Black Country,' an area which encompassed West Bromwich, Dudley and Wolverhampton. 'Moving from group to group had helped me further my knowledge of the blues, then I got in with a lot of Jamaicans and I started to like Blue Beat and Ska.' Robert became a Mod, and even had French style short hair cut, inspired by Steve Marriott of The Small Faces. Says Robert: 'Steve was the master of contemporary white blues.' Not only were the singers improving to Marriott-Winwood standards, but the guitarists and drummers were getting better too. Working alongside Robert in the Crawling King Snakes was drummer John Bonham, who matched Robert's wild reputation with his own notoriety as the loudest drummer in town. It was the first time Bonham and Plant had met and their paths would cross again before finally teaming up in Led Zeppelin.

Robert spent some six years in virtual obscurity playing in these small time groups but attempts were at last made to enter him into the world of recording and promote Robert as an artist who deserved wider recognition. He was asked to join a group called The Tennessee Teens, a three piece Tamla Motown influenced group. Robert was now aged eighteen and when he joined, the group changed their name to Listen. It was 1966 and Robert was at last 'discovered' by a CBS Records talent scout. He was signed by CBS who released three Robert Plant singles, all of which have become collector's items.

The first was issued in late 1966 under the name of Listen but was actually Robert backed by session musicians. The A-side was 'You Better Run' and the B-side, co-written by Robert, was 'Everybody's Gonna Say'. 'You Better Run', a Young Rascals song, was simultaneously recorded by another Midlands

● *Robert raving in San Diego, 1972.*

group The N'Betweens, who later achieved fame as Slade. For a brief period The N'Betweens lead singer, Noddy Holder, worked as a roadie with Plant's group, Listen, driving them around the Black Country in his father's window cleaning van. Robert's first solo release under his own name was a cover version of an Italian ballad called 'Our Song' backed with 'Laughing, Crying, Laughing', released by CBS in March 1967. The A-side was a slow, heavily orchestrated ballad with bluesy vocals with some typical Plant style 'Ooh baby' ejaculations. It sold some 800 copies. 'When 'Our Song' was released I walked around embarrassed for a bit, but now it's great to hear and smile at,' says Robert about his first stab at a solo career. At least it proved he could handle a variety of material. 'All the copies I saw were demos with a big A on the label. Making a record was a big step. Once you'd got a piece of music on plastic, if it represents you, that's good, and you can take it from there. At the time there were a lot of great groups around . . . The In Crowd, the English group called The Birds (not to be confused with The Byrds), Graham Bond's Organisation, Georgie Fame . . . this was the time of The Whiskey club in Birmingham.'

The third single, Robert's second under his own name, was issued in September 1967, and was called 'Long Time Coming' coupled with 'I've Got A Secret'. This time Robert emitted a piercing scream at the end of the A-side; it sold enough to make the local magazine's Top Twenty.

'Originally I went to London on the understanding that I could record a cover version of a track called 'Incense' by The Angelos,' says Robert. 'It was a sort of challenge but when I got there, the people in charge had a preconceived idea of how I should be presented to the public. It was just so antiquated . . . their idea of how anyone should be. It was just ridiculous but I'd signed a piece of paper which led to three very strange records. The only copies ever sold were the ones my mum bought.' All three appeared in bootleg form on a 1981 LP titled *Solo Performances* which also included the soundtrack music Jimmy Page wrote in the seventies for the Kenneth Anger film *Lucifer Rising*.

In attempts to build up Robert's image, the CBS press release that accompanied the singles claimed that Robert played violin, piano, organ and guitar. No mention was made of the washboard. In 1966, the year he signed his first record contract, he also met his girlfriend Maureen Wilson who would later become his wife. They met at a Georgie Fame concert, distinguished chiefly by the fact that Georgie Fame didn't turn up; Maureen would later prove a tower of strength when Robert's career hit a rough patch. His newest group was The Band Of Joy, which had been influenced by Birmingham's West Indian community and played some blue beat and ska. They seemed to revel in choosing obscure material and there were endless changes in personnel. At an early stage even Robert was sacked, for being 'too outspoken'. One of the first line-ups of The Band Of Joy included, Robert on vocals, Chris Brown (keyboards), Peter 'Plug' Robinson (drums)

● *Peter Grant emerges from limo. Robert sets off to work.*

and Vernon Pireira (guitar). It was Pireira, a cousin of Robert's future wife Maureen, who persuaded Robert not to abandon singing after his group Listen disbanded. Sadly Pireira was killed in 1976 in a motorway crash with other members of his group, Possessed.

In 1966 The Band Of Joy played in Wolverhampton on Sunday nights at The Ship And Rainbow, now the site of a local brewery office. They were put into a residency by Nita Anderson Presentations, a local booking agency and drew capacity crowds of around six hundred a night. Nita recalls a phone call from Robert's mother asking her to 'look after my son's career.'

Robert stayed with the agency for three years but the Ship And Rainbow residency ended when the landlord took offence to the lyrics of 'Spoonful Of Sugar' a blues song which he thought referred to LSD. There were also complaints that the group's music sounded like 'An Indian dirge.' Says Robert: 'The Band Of Joy had started off shakily, doing things like Prince Buster's 'Ten Commandments Of Man' with toy machine guns and immitation fights on stage. We had flashing TV sets, lights and we wore tail coats. These ideas were copied by another local group The Move.'

Although Robert was sacked by the group, he hung onto the name and recruited a new Band Of Joy with bassist Paul Lockey. Explains Lockey: 'Robert had a semi-pro group in West Bromwich called, Robert Plant And The Band of Joy, working at

'It was an incessant search, constantly to develop musical taste'
ROBERT PLANT

weekends.' The line-up then included Kevin Gammond (guitar), Chris Brown (keyboards), and Johnny Trickett (drums). 'In a later line up we recruited a loud flash drummer called John Bonham after getting him drunk one night,' says Paul. 'We went on to play a range of venues including the Midlands colleges and The Penthouse on Snow Hill, Birmingham, where we held a post concern seance in which we "Got through." The building was on the site of an old cemetery.' The group experienced all the horrors attendant on gigging around the country. One such horror was when they travelled home non-stop from Lands End for a Saturday night dance and their Commer van, heavily laden with gear, broke down on the way to York. But despite it all they were quite successful, supporting acts such as, Geno Washington and the Ram Jam Band, and the Pretty Things, and managing three tours of Scotland.

In another version of The Band Of Joy in 1967, Flower Power was a strong influence. They painted their faces. and wore kaftans, beads and bells. 'It went all right for a while, but we were frightening our audiences to death,' says Robert. This version of the band was having a hard job converting the Provinces to the kind of West Coast music that London had only just discovered. Robert was particularly enamoured of Love, featuring Arthur Lee and of course Moby Grape. They managed to get down to the hub of the 'Underground' movement, playing at Middle Earth in London on the same bill as Ten Years After and Fairport Convention. Although they earned sixty pounds for a booking, with all the overheads it still wasn't enough to make a living. Maureen kept Robert going with the money from her day job. Robert even had to start labouring to bring in more cash. He thought he might end up on the dole. 'But I wasn't going to give up. For a while I was living off Maureen, God bless her. Then I did some road making to earn some bread. I actually laid half the asphalt on West Bromwich High Street. All it did for me was to give be 6/2d per hour, an emergency tax code and big biceps. All the navvies would call me 'the pop singer.' It was really funny.'

Guitarist Kevin Gammond who used the name 'Carlisle Egypt' in later versions of The Band Of Joy recalled the music they played in those days. It certainly wasn't hippie trippy stuff, despite the kaftans. He was in the line up with Robert, John Bonham and Paul Lockey. 'It was the flower power era but the act

● *Flying the flag, in Newcastle.*

was hard and aggressive with the emphasis on loud, heavy blues. We played at several noted London venues including Middle Earth and The Speakeasy, as well as youth clubs and Midlands ballrooms.' Kevin has tapes of the group which they recorded on 8-track machines at Regent Sound Studios in London. They feature a song called 'Adriatic Seaview' and an original blues number 'Sweet Mary'. Another track was called 'Memory Lane'. 'That was really quite funny,' recalls Robert. 'It was about a chick on the back of a motorbike with a chrome horse between her legs . . . sort of an early version of 'Wanton Song' from Led Zeppelin's *Physical Graffiti*'. Other cuts recorded by the group at Regent Sound were a version of 'Hey Joe', the traditional song that Jimi Hendrix made famous, and 'What's That Sound' a Jim Messina song Buffalo Springfield had recorded and which Zeppelin later played on some of their earliest concerts. At this time Robert went to the Marquee studios to record some demos including a version of Elvis Presley's 'One Night'. He was there at the request of Move manager. Tony Secunda, who had thought of signing Robert to Regal Zonophone, a plan which was dropped under pressure from the label's boss Denny Cordell.

In early 1968 The Band Of Joy toured Britain, supporting Tim Rose (who had a hit with his own version of 'Hey Joe'), alongside Aynsley Dunbar's Retaliation. Robert's group acted as Tim Rose's back up. In their own set they played Rose's song 'Morning Dew' and Rose and Robert would occasionally sing it as a duet.

Their keyboard player Chris Brown was in both the first and last versions of The Band Of Joy. He told Howard Mylett: 'The first time I met Robert he was at

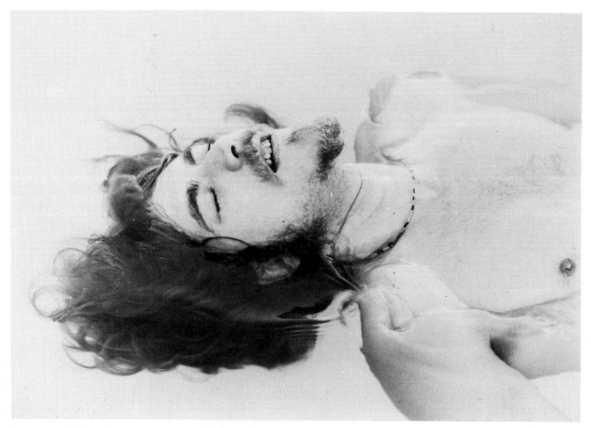

● *Searching for fresh supplies of mudsharks.*

Vernon Pireira's house. He came home black from digging up the roads. We received star treatment at the YMCA in Kirkaldy, but at the Saturday night dance at the Victoria Hall in Selkirk, a drunken reveller threw a poorly aimed meat pie at Robert who dodged it and hurled back a well chosen comment.

'Robert used to use my home telephone and got calls from bluesman Alexis Korner who he had met and befriended at the Speakeasy club in London. At the Speakeasy the music we played was very loud blues, with John's drum kit at the front of the stage. We played really well to an audience that included Paul McCartney and Frank Zappa. Drinks were a pound each and we drank Cokes unless a celebrity sent a drink up to us.'

Robert remembers gigs at the Speakeasy, then the 'In' club for the music business, situated in London's Margaret Street. 'Although we took turns driving the group van, and John handled the equipment, one night he was drunk and reversed into a railing losing the door handle. When he went to open the door with a shovel he saw Keith Moon holding a champagne party inside his Rolls Royce, parked outside the Speak. He held Keith in great esteem and didn't want to be seen struggling to open the van door.'

Robert found it difficult to take their flirtation with flower power seriously; they painted their faces long before Arthur Brown had a hit with 'Fire'. There was a fat bass player who was dressed in kaftan and bells who used to come running on and dived straight into the audience bellowing. I howled so much with laughter I couldn't do anything. It was absurd . . . I thought it was time for another Band Of Joy and that's when Kevin Gammond, John and Paul Lockey came in. The group used to travel to Redditch to pick John up. We did arrangements of 'She Has Funny Cars,' and 'Plastic Fantastic Lover'.

The money improved when they played London and began to earn £100 a night, although there was one gig in Scotland for just twenty pounds. It was this last version of The Band Of Joy which was the most positive and held the happiest memories for Robert. Their repertoire included songs by Howlin' Wolf, Muddy Waters and Sonny Boy Williamson, as well Grateful Dead tunes. They were managed by Mike Dolan and the line-up was still prone to changes, depending on how much money was offered for each gig. John Bonham suggested the group be billed as The Band Of Joy Featuring John Bonham, which led to a fight among the musicians at Glamorgan Polytechnic. Says Robert: 'I remember another night when John got angry with the guitar player at a gig in Exeter and he played the drums standing up all night. John always said he was the best drummer in the world, and of course we later found out that he was.'

CHAPTER FIVE
FLY, ZEPPELIN, FLY

The late sixties was the age of the Super Group. It is a phrase that has fallen into disuse after being much derided and misunderstood and has become synonymous with power politics and commercial greed, where disparate talents are linked together for no other reason than to present a profit making package. This wasn't the original concept. Apart from the phrase making useful headline material, it exemplified the sort of union musicians dreamed about, when hemmed in by the stultifying incompetence of their fellow players.

Many of the groups achieving fame during the boom years of pop had grown up together. They were friends who had made the grade, more by luck than musicianship and so there were often duffers being carried in the ranks; stoned rhythm guitarists and tardy drummers. It was natural for the best of the emerging bunch, who took playing more seriously, to cast envious eyes and wish that somehow they could get it together with their peers, in the country, or better still on-stage at the next mammoth outdoor festival; and so there came into being Cream, Traffic and Humble Pie. These 'dream bands' gave shelter to the disaffected, promised musical freedom and, of course, there was always the chance of a big advance from a record company. Logistically it all made sense, even if the supposed benefits of such alliances, oft proved illusory.

The first manifestations of the super group concept (celebrated in the early rock movie 'Super Session'), were fun and productive; witness the success of Cream, which starred three of the finest players of the day, Eric Clapton, Ginger Baker and Jack Bruce. It was the rock version of the 'What if' principle applied by jazz promoter Norman Granz, who thought 'what if I pitch Charlie Parker against Johnny Hodges, or Buddy Rich with Art Tatum?' The results could be uneven, but always intriguing and often surprisingly good.

Led Zeppelin was very nearly a supergroup. The original plan, long kept secret, to team up Jimmy Page with Steve Marriott, John Entwistle and Keith Moon would undoubtedly have been sensational. But it would probably have resulted in the destruction of all of them within a matter of weeks as temperaments and egos clashed. They were good friends with much mutual respect between them, but after a few days on the road, they'd be throwing each other and not the obligatory hotel furniture into the pool. Led Zeppelin as it finally emerged, proved a superbly balanced band, immensely powerful and very suc-

● *Jimmy takes you higher.*

cessful, but it was not a 'super group'. Only one of the four man crew was a 'face' and he was something of a mystery man.

Jimmy Page, coming out of the studios, had thrown in his lot with the Yardbirds, and accepted a return to touring. But he found himself with a band on its way out, and most of its final appearances were abroad, away from the all devouring gaze of the English weekly music press. The 'New Yardbirds' was actually Jimmy using up some of the old band's remaining dates, while preparing to launch Led Zeppelin. He finally explained the mystery to me by turning up unannounced at the *Melody Maker* office one lunch time. I subsequently wrote a story comparing the disappearance of The Yardbirds to the fate of the crew of the Marie Celeste. Jimmy told me: 'We

didn't do any gigs in England for two years, so no wonder we lost popularity. But just before we split we did a couple of colleges that were really fantastic. I was knocked out. We were a happy group and used to get on well socially until we got on-stage and Keith lost all enthusiasm. I used to say "Come on chaps, let's make an effort," but it had all gone. When they split I think it did us a favour because the new chaps are only aged nineteen and are full of enthusiasm. It was getting a bit of a trial in the old group.'

'His voice was too great to be undiscovered'
JIMMY PAGE

I first heard about the New Yardbirds on a trip to Sweden, reporting on the boisterous activities of the pop group called Marmalade for the *Melody Maker*. There, pinned on a wall back-stage at the Tivoli Gardens, Stockholm in September 1968, was a poster detailing visiting groups. 'The New Yardbirds' it said. 'But I thought they had broken up,' said Dean Ford, the Marmalade's singer. As it turned out we just missed seeing a bit of history in the making. We would have been the first to see this new band featuring Jimmy Page with Robert Plant.

At this stage Jimmy still wasn't sure whether to go on using the name 'Yardbirds' and no mention had been made of Led Zeppelin: 'I thought I'd never get a band together. I've always shied off leadership in the past because of all that ego thing. I didn't want The Yardbirds to break up but in the end it was too much of a headache. I just wanted to play guitar basically, but Keith Relf always had this great thing of being overshadowed by Jeff which was nonsense. It was great fun when we had the two lead guitars. It's refreshing to know that today you can go out and form a group to play the music you like and people will listen. It's what musicians have been waiting for twenty years.'

Jimmy's dream came together quite quickly in the wake of The Yardbirds break up. Jimmy had a bass player, John Paul Jones, who also played keyboards, but his first attempts at recruiting a singer were stymied. He wanted Terry Reid, then a rising star with a rasping, powerful voice. Terry could also play guitar, but had just signed with Mickie Most to be promoted as a solo artist. It was Terry who recommended Robert Plant for the job.

By this stage Robert's own career seemed to be running into a brick wall. The Band Of Joy had resolutely played whatever music took their fancy,

● LEFT: *Zeppelin blasting at Earl's Court.*

with a heavy West Coast influence, mixed with traditional blues. Says Robert: 'There were very few other groups around at the time who were doing the same thing, but gaining acceptance was hard and coming from Birmingham didn't help. The Band Of Joy was a cradle for everything I really enjoyed in music. I believed that if I loved these numbers, then by playing them sincerely the rest of the people who heard them would enjoy them too. Instead of that it turned out to be a failure in the end.

'Everyone was expecting us to go on and do Cream numbers which I had no intention of doing. No one gave two hoots and no one wanted to know. We had a great time but financially the band couldn't survive. 'None of the band wanted to leave the comforts and security of home in the Midlands and risk moving to London and centre of the music business. Robert's manager said they were all hopeless and would never make it and Robert was also advised that he 'couldn't sing.' The Band Of Joy broke up. John Bonham went off to tour with Tim Rose, and Robert sang for a while with Alexis Korner, whose own band Blues Incorporated had long since gone. They gigged together around Birmingham and also did shows at Kirkaldy YMCA and Middle Earth, still a hippie stronghold, in Covent Garden. Robert told the *New Musical Express* in April 1970 about his time with Alexis. 'I was working immediately before Led Zeppelin with Alexis Korner and we were in the process of recording an album with a pianist called Steve Miller. A very fluid thing . . . nothing definitely set up. We had a wonderful time and we were going to do a few festivals in Germany.'

A remnant of that collaboration can be heard on the Alexis Korner double album *Bootleg Him* (Metronome DALP 2/3101). Amidst a mass of desultory jam sessions, the one track featuring Robert shines out with dazzling brilliance. It's a simple slow blues called 'Operator' with rumbling boogie piano and Alexis' gently urging acoustic guitar. It provides an insight into Robert's development as this early stage. He comes on with fantastic power and confidence, a fully formed blues singer with all his skills and devices wrapped up and ready to go. The faint interjections by Alexis seem ludicrous, as Robert storms into the song taking deep breaths to emphasise the key words and expelling them with the force of an American freight locomotive pulling away – with a hundred wagons – up an incline. No wonder Jimmy Page was astounded when he first heard Robert sing. He was excited by the vocal prowess, and mildly astonished that such a singer could remain hidden for so long.

The gigs with Alexis Korner were fun and Robert was even allowed to play some of his favourite West Coast songs, like 'White Rabbit'. But then it was back to Birmingham to sing with the local group Hobbstweedle. It was at a teachers' training college gig with Hobbstweedle that he was seen by Jimmy and Peter Grant, at the behest of Terry Reid. 'I'd met Terry at one or two gigs in the Band Of Joy Days,' recalls Robert.

- OPPOSITE TOP: *Jimmy in '2050' gear.*

- BELOW: *This bass drum is bigger than the both of us.*

- ABOVE: *Robert checks out John Paul's piano.*

- RIGHT: *'Next question'. Jimmy fends off an interviewer.*

● *Getting into the acoustic set.*

Robert was in London on his mission to involve Tony Secunda in his career, when Terry Reid told him he'd heard that The Yardbirds singer had left, and suggested Robert tried to get into the scene. Robert knew the band did a lot of work in America where he thought audiences would be more appreciative. 'Naturally I was very interested,' says Robert. Messages were passed to and fro and then it was arranged for Robert to travel to Jimmy Page's home, an old boathouse in Pangbourne, Berkshire, for a meeting. On the way he found himself in dire straits. 'It was a real desperation scene. I had nowhere else to go. There I was with my suitcase getting off the train and suddenly this old woman started slapping my face and shouting about my hair. Well I was staggered . . . so I called a cop and he said it was my own fault for having long hair. So much for British justice.' Robert finally arrived at Jimmy's place and after browsing through his record collection, realised they had the same musical tastes. Each album he pulled out was by someone he liked. 'I knew then we'd click. Nobody in Britain wanted to know us, but Jimmy told us it'd be different in the States.'

This sudden and unexpected introduction to Jimmy Page meant hope for two people both burning with ambition and raring to go. 'The group really woke me up from inertia,' said Robert later. 'Years and years with no success can really bring you down. Peter and Jimmy were as adamant as I was about the music that I wanted to play but they also had application and experience. Peter had push and Jimmy was a craftsman. He moulded me, and we both hit the same spot on the dial. If our musical tastes hadn't been similar, we'd have gone our own ways, but all was not in vain.' It was a discovery for Jimmy also. 'His voice was too great to be undiscovered,' said Jimmy. 'It was like a primeval wail. When I auditioned him and heard him sing I immediately thought there must be something wrong with him personality wise, or that he had to be impossible to work with, because I just couldn't understand why he hadn't become a big name yet. I thought Robert was fantastic.'

The proposed new band, however, was still in a state of flux. Chris Dreja had dropped out to be replaced by John Paul Jones, and the original choice for a drummer, B. J. Wilson was unavailable. During his trip to Pangbourne Robert told Jimmy about his friend John Bonham. Jimmy was interested. Robert hitch-hiked back home (he couldn't afford the £1.50 train fare and Jimmy doesn't appear to have lent him the money), and tracked Bonham down. Robert was full of enthusiasm for the project and told Bonzo, 'you must come!' But Bonzo was less than keen. He was earning good money with Tim Rose, he was featured in a drum solo, and he also had tempting offers from Joe Cocker and Chris Farlowe (the latter job went to another Birmingham lad, Carl Palmer).

Eventually John was persuaded – he knew the music would be good if nothing else. A batch of telegrams did have to be sent northwards before Bonham finally showed up. Robert, Jimmy and Peter Grant all went to see him play with Tim Rose at the Country Club, a popular gig in London's West Hampstead. Rehearsals were called and Robert met John Paul Jones for the first time. One of the first numbers they played was 'As Long As I Have You' a Garnett Mimms song Robert used to sing in the Band Of Joy. The other tune was Jimmy's favourite from The Yardbirds 'Train Kept A Rollin.' As soon as they began to play in a small, hot, airless studio, they began to smile and laugh as they realised it was going to work. Robert described the experience as 'Incredibly illuminating,' as everyone was asked to contribute ideas and discuss the arrangements and choice of material. Although Plant and Bonham were new boys compared to the other two, and slightly in awe of their professional status, they felt equals in the challenging task of creating a new band. 'The chemistry between us was immediate and perfect, as were the astrological forces at work', says Robert. The band was playing the kind of music they all knew and loved. And there was no one to hold them back, no one who would be burned by their excellence or intimidated by their energy and youth. No one, that is, within the band. The outside world would react in all manner of unpredictable ways when the full force of the group began to hit.

Now they were together, Peter Grant could go to work. Peter was one of the great characters of the pop world. A mountainous figure who had been a wrestler and a film actor, Peter knew the business inside out. After useful training in the army and later in a holiday camp, he could knock this bunch of wild-eyed youngsters into a team.

Peter had once worked as a bouncer at the 2Is coffee bar in Soho where he met Mickie Most who also worked there, as a waiter. Later he worked with promoter Don Arden and was tour manager for Gene Vincent. He saw how many hard working rock veterans were ripped off and was determined that any band he managed would get the money that was due to them. Peter later toured America with The Animals when they were managed by Mike Jeffery, and then took over The Yardbirds from Simon Napier-Bell. He booked them into important gigs like The Fillmore, in San Francisco, run by Bill Graham. He could see that The Yardbirds were a great band and had tremendous possibilities, but they were not strong enough to take advantage of the rapidly growing US rock concert circuit. A new band with Jimmy Page at the helm would undoubtedly clean up. He was annoyed when England seemed to spurn his new creation, and impatiently whisked them off to the States. His first important act however was to sign the band for a huge advance (for the times) to Atlantic Records.

The signing was not without the drama that came to surround the group's whole career. Epic records who had The Yardbirds thought they would be signing The New Yardbirds. While discussions were going ahead, Peter casually dropped into the conversation the news that he had just signed the band to Atlantic for $200,000. The label, famed for its blues, jazz and soul heritage had just been getting into signing British rock acts like Yes. They took on The New Yardbirds without even having heard or seen them play, largely on the strength of recommendations from singer Dusty Springfield to Atlantic's Jerry Wexler.

Three weeks after their first rehearsals the band set off for their ten day Scandinavian tour. But they couldn't go on calling themselves The New Yardbirds, even if it pleased promoters. There came the anguished business of finding a name that would please everybody and yet have distinction. They considered calling themselves The Mad Dogs. Said Jimmy, 'The name wasn't as important as the music. We could have called ourselves The Vegetables or The Potatoes. I was quite keen about Led Zeppelin ... it seemed to fit the bill.' There was some early confusion about whether it should be 'Lead' as in 'lead balloon' but then this could sound like 'lead' as in 'lead guitar.' However Led Zeppelin it was; resur-

● *Jimmy in yokel's hat, Bath Festival, 1970.*

rected from the one thought up by Keith Moon and John Entwistle some months earlier.

The band made its British debut at Surrey University on October 15, 1968. They then played at London's Marquee club, which announced even more confusingly 'The British Debut Of The Yardbirds' on October 18. The following day they played Liverpool University as Led Zeppelin and from then on they were billed only as Led Zeppelin. They played again at the Marquee under their new name and were given favourable reviews, many commenting on the cocksure young singer, who some thought looked like a Greek god with his curly hair and classical good looks. The combination of brazen sex appeal and thunderous approach to the blues seemed almost too much for the earnest British fans, supping their light ales and wondering if this was authentically valid.

The sets already featured the song 'Dazed And Confused', with Jimmy using the violin bow on his guitar strings, and 'Robert answering the guitar phrases with spine tingling yells. All this would have to be captured on album. The band had already had some recording experience together when they backed American singer, P. J. Proby, on his album *Three Week Hero*. With Robert on harmonica, poor old Proby was swept away by the power-house backing – most obvious on the track 'Jim's Blues'. Proby, despite his Southern origins, patently couldn't sing the blues, at least not with the same conviction as Robert. Proby struggled to scream out a few words, while the Zeppelin crew threatened to blow him out of the studio.

They began work on their own LP at Olympic Studios, on their return from Sweden, and in two-and-a-half weeks and in thirty studio hours they laid down the tracks for one of the finest rock albums of all time *Led Zeppelin*. Even while he was busy with his new project Jimmy just found time to finish off some session work, playing on Al Stewart's *Love Chronicles* album and Joe Cocker's 'With A Little Help From My Friends' a big hit single, and graced by Jimmy's 'haunting introduction' – a phrase that would crop up in Zeppelin work.

While the album was in the pipeline, awaiting release in Britain and America in the New Year, the band carried on gigging, their reputation spreading like wildfire. They played at The Roundhouse in Chalk Farm, on November 9, 1968, got paid £150 and were given a tumultuous reception. The same day Robert got married to Maureen. 'That was our honeymoon, playing at The Roundhouse!' said Robert.

In December 1968 they played several dates in England before leaving for America where they made their debut in Denver, Colorado on December 26. Their impact on American audiences was stunning. US fans were much more demonstrative than their English counterparts, whooping, yelling and shaking their heads. It was thrilling for the band, and proof that they had all taken the right decision. It was

● *Jimmy talks to Chris Welch at Swan Song.*

the start of twelve tempestuous years together. There would be triumphs and disasters. They would become rich and famous. 'They were all millionaires after their first year,' said one of their aides. Money poured in from the sales of their first album, which went straight into the Top Ten in America and stayed there for the rest of the year; and although many of their first club dates were poorly paid, hangovers

'I knew then we'd click'
ROBERT PLANT

from bookings made before the record was a hit, eventually they began to earn huge sums from extensive tours.

British fans began to feel somewhat left out of the excitement. The album wasn't even released in the UK until March, but the reviews, which began to appear in the music press the following month, were nearly all ecstatic. 'Zeppelin are a gas!' yelled the headlines. The Zeppelin camp were still miffed that the media had seemed to ignore their arrival on the scene, forgetting that, in those halcyon days, new groups were arriving by the bus load every week and so the sorting of wheat from chaff sometimes went awry. Suffice to say the *Melody Maker* as early as December 1968 had predicted that Led Zeppelin would be the biggest name in rock in the coming year.

Anyone kicking themselves at having missed seeing the band 'live' at the London pub and club gigs, could catch up by listening to the album. It had the pace and vitality that a band could normally only generate 'live'. Maybe it was Page's burgeoning ability as a producer or the skill of engineer Glyn Johns, but between them and the band they created a vibrant sound that was a revelation. It was as if the grey blankets of traditional recording techniques (as applied to rock groups) had been stripped away and the resonance of the guitars, drums and vocals could be heard with a pristine clarity and almost brutal power. The first album and its successor *Led Zeppelin II*, released in October 1969, both had these qualities which means they hardly sound dated today when many other albums from the same period are depressingly flat.

Tracks on the first album included; 'Dazed And Confused', 'Good Times Bad Times', 'Babe I'm Gonna Leave You', 'You Shook Me', 'Your Time Is Gonna Come', 'Black Mountain Side', 'Communication Breakdown', 'I Can't Quit You Baby' and 'How Many More Times'. There was a wide range of styles, from folk to blues and rock. They were loud and they could play long and fast, but that wasn't the whole story and it always baffled and annoyed the group when some critics called them a heavy metal band who could only be appreciated while stoned.

Jimmy was determined from the start of the band to show they could play acoustically as well as electrically, and he felt their intentions were clearly set out on the first LP. He discussed the making of the album with John Tobler, for the BBC Radio One series *The Guitar Greats*. He explained that they were able to make the album at speed because they were full of excitement from some 'live' dates. 'I wanted the band to come through with something that was hard hitting dynamite that other musicians would respect as well, but would be so good that everyone in the band would feel committed to it, which was how it went in fact, and what was great was that such a respect was built up between the four of us for each other.

'We rehearsed quite a lot within the framework of the numbers, but the full construction, the embellishments, the overdubs and certain lyrics, like the verses on 'Communication Breakdown', where there had just been one chorus, were all added.'

Jimmy admitted he had built up a stock of riff ideas while he was with The Yardbirds, when they played free form versions of 'Smokestack Lightnin'.' 'Obviously I wasn't going to throw all that away, as

● *'Low key gig', Southampton, 1971.*

they hadn't been recorded, so I remodelled those riffs and used them again. The bowing on 'How Many More Times' and 'Good Times, Bad Times' was an extension of what I'd been working on with The Yardbirds, although I'd never had that much chance to go to town with it and see how far one could stretch the bowing technique on record and obviously for anyone who saw the band, it became quite a little showpiece in itself. It was really enjoyable to do. People used to remark on it, so obviously they enjoyed watching it.' Jimmy thought that the technique produced some remarkably effective, and highly musical sounds, with the depth of a 'cello.

Each member of the band nade a vital contribution to the album, and Jimmy told how 'Good Times, Bad Times' came out of a John Paul Jones bass guitar riff, and featured some of John Bonham's finest playing. 'It really knocked everybody sideways when they heard the bass drum pattern, because I think everyone was laying bets that Bonzo was using two bass drums, but he only had one. 'Dazed And Confused' came from The Yardbirds, and that was my showcase, show-off bit with the bow, and that was one example, I guess, of how everything but the kitchen sink was in that first album, from my end I think that was something I did consciously, because I started off all the numbers on that LP, and I did a lot of different things with different instruments, leaning heavily on some of the ideas that I'd developed with The Yardbirds, because I knew they were things I'd

- ABOVE: *Ready for Knebworth, 1979.*
- LEFT: *Robert browsing through 'Groupie'.*
- RIGHT: *Off to the Far East.*

● *Interplay.*

come up with myself rather than riffs Eric or Jeff had done. I'd always been interested in every facet of and approach to guitar playing, from flamenco to classical to fifties rock'n'roll. I just love every aspect of guitar playing.'

On 'Babe I'm Gonna Leave You' and 'Your Time Is Gonna Come' Jimmy used to pedal steel guitar for the first time, aiming for the sort of sound Chuck Berry had achieved on tunes like 'Deep Feeling'. 'It was OK on 'Babe I'm Gonna Leave You' but on 'Your Time Is Gonna Come' the intonation was extremely suspect. That one tried to get a bit too ambitious.' Nevertheless the quirky sound produced by the pedal steel only added to the air of mystery and menace as Robert chanted the chorus and went into the second verse. The moment when Jimmy's acoustic guitar interrupted the dying moments of 'Gonna Come' to launch into the unexpected delights of 'Black Mountain Side' was one of the touches that made the album so intriguing and ultimately satisfying. Instantly popular was the fast moving 'Communication Breakdown', a quick burst of energy and their answer to The Who's 'My Generation'. Said Jimmy, 'The idea of 'Communication Breakdown' was to have a really raw hard hitting number. It's hard to describe the feeling of playing those numbers at the time, but it was so exciting and electrifying to be part of it, and that one was always so good to play, so staccato, just a knock out to do.'

The album soon went to gold and in America the fans flocked to see them in a string of concerts from coast to coast. There the band took full advantage of the nationwide network of rock radio stations, the underground music press, and the general swift acceptance of rock music as an important arm of the entertainment industry. In Britain, everything seemed slow, antiquated and lack-lustre. Although the fans were by now just as enthusiastic as the Americans for Led Zeppelin, Peter Grant still had to patiently explain to the promoters that they were now Led Zeppelin and not The New Yardbirds as they were booked into Mothers' Club, Birmingham, Cooks Ferry Inn, Edmonton, and Klook's Kleek, Hampstead.

The group were working flat out for the whole of 1969 and it seemed they had taken on a twenty-four hour a day job. They had to try recording tracks for their next album in between an endless succession of concerts. It was only when they paused for breath that the size and scope of their success began to penetrate. 'That success came as a massive surprise' said Jimmy. 'It didn't hit me until the day we were presented with our first gold record. I thought "My goodness! A gold record!" We were a completely untried group of people who got together in the space of a few weeks to produce an album which really had only one ingredient that we were sure of – genuine enthusiasm.'

It wasn't long before such success began to breed resentment. Even while some critics were shouting from the rooftops; 'Led Zeppelin are the new Cream . . . they are the biggest happening of 1969!', others were grumbling 'Hype!' It was true the album was sent in advance to local radio stations, for them to play before the band arrived in town, but this was normal practice. And in England most of the numbers were too long to get any radio play at all. They did, however, make a rare TV appearance on BBC TV's *How It Is* standing in for The Flying Burrito Brothers, who had gone missing. The year was full of 'firsts' for the band, like playing at Newport Jazz Festival, appearing in the British made film *Super Session* (which also included Eric Clapton, Stephen Stills, Buddy Miles and Buddy Guy), and prestigious gigs at Bath Festival, The Royal Albert Hall in London and Carnegie Hall, in New York.

By the summer the group were earning around thirty thousand dollars per concert, on their headlining American tour which included a percentage of the 'gate' money. This further incensed some observers. Responded Jimmy, 'For anyone to imply that Led Zeppelin were prefabricated or hyped-up on a gullible public is grossly unfair. You can't compute or calculate for a situation like that or the chemistry which arises when you put together a band. We could have been a bum group. No one ever knows until you start working together. And if you're good, things start to happen.'

Proving that they hadn't burnt themselves out in the glorious burst of energy that produced their first album, *Led Zeppelin II*, released in October 1969, was packed with strong songs. The tracks, recorded in scattered locations and mixed at Olympic included

● *Jimmy bows out.*

'Whole Lotta Love', 'What Is And What Should Never Be', 'The Lemon Song', 'Thank You', 'Heartbreaker', 'Living Loving Maid (She's A Woman)', 'Ramble On', 'Moby Dick' and 'Bring It On Home'. There wasn't quite the same eerie presence of the first album, but the riffs were just as exciting. 'Whole Lotta Love' became an instant hit and although the group refused to allow it to be released as a single in Britain (they argued that the album would sell as well as a single if the track remained exclusive), it became the theme tune to BBC TV's *Top Of The Pops*, although it was not the version recorded by the band. Jimmy Page had conceived the grinding, sonorous riff that finally established the band's image in the public mind. 'The riff came from me,' says Jimmy, 'but don't ask me where it came from before that, because it just came out of thin air, as nearly all riffs do. It was pretty infectious, although it's being on *Top Of The Pops* every week killed it over here, which was a drag.'

Jimmy felt that the music on *Led Zeppelin II* once again showed the band could play in a variety of moods, and one of the most interesting was 'Heart Breaker' with Robert shouting over an insistent rolling bass and guitar pattern, broken up by key changes and an angular guitar solo chorus followed by changes of tempo. Says Jimmy: 'It wasn't just like hitting a riff and going on and on at it at the same intensity, it was a question of light and shade and dynamics, and it would be really loud one minute, and so soft that a pin could drop and be heard the next.'

By now Robert Plant was becoming more involved in lyric writing. Explained Jimmy, 'In the early days I was writing the lyrics as well as the music, because Robert hadn't written before, and it took a lot of ribbing and teasing to actually get him into writing, which was funny. And then, on the second LP, he wrote the words of 'Thank You'.' This was written by Robert as a tribute to Maureen and all the help she had given him in the lean years. There was no danger now of Robert ever having to go back to navvying. The success that swept over them that first year left them breathless and changed their lifestyles for ever. He bought himself a farmhouse in the Midlands, tilled the soil, sowed crops and tended his goats. After the wild life on the road in America surrounded by adoring fans and groupies, Robert could get back to reality and muck out the stables. The peace of the countryside seemed like a glorious relief from the endless flights and mad dashes between hotels, gigs and airports, intermingled with the adrenalin pumping experience of nightly concerts, with all their attendant uproar. Said Robert, 'The worst thing in the world is to rush. Being on the road so much has taught me that. All I want to do is sit back and take it easy. The farm calms me down. When I'm away on-stage I'm so into it that if I didn't have the farm I'd go mad.'

CHAPTER SIX
GOOD TIMES, BAD TIMES

Led Zeppelin towered over the seventies. They were the most powerful and popular rock band of the age, whose success in terms of albums and tickets sold outstripped that of The Rolling Stones. As a live act they ran rings around the opposition, with a mixture of blues and rock styles that managed to be both traditional in outlook yet thoroughly modern. There were other highly successful bands it was true – the early seventies was a time of great expansion, with Black Sabbath, Grand Funk Railroad, ELP, Tes, Wings, Deep Purple and The Who all dominating the scene. Zeppelin, however, were in a class of their own. They had the most fans, played the biggest concerts and presented the most united front, with no dissent over their musical direction.

In 1970 Led Zeppelin could do no wrong. They played at Bath Festival in June that year, with Jimmy wearing a yokel's hat and old overcoat, a kind of

reaction against the satin clad flower power era, and an attempt to cool down the heat and excitement they were generating at every turn. They played for three hours and took five encores. It marked the ultimate breakthrough of acceptance in their home country and Robert in particular was thrilled. Later that year they toured the cities of Germany, and having opened in Cincinatti that August, completed their sixth sell-out tour of America.

After a brief holiday, the band played two concerts in Madison Square Garden, New York, which earned them over $100,000. Gold albums kept on coming, including one for a million sales of *Led Zeppelin II* in Europe, and another for advance orders on *Led Zeppelin III* which was released in October. Tracks on this included 'Immigrant Song', 'Friends', 'Celebration Day', 'Since I've Been Loving You', 'Out On The Tiles', 'Gallows Pole', 'Tangerine', 'That's The Way', 'Bron-Y-Aur-Stomp', and 'Hats Off To (Roy) Harper'.

Led Zeppelin III was recorded earlier in the year, and by the end of 1970 the band had already fin-

● *In transit: Jones, Page, Bonham, Plant.*

● *Smokin' strings. American tour, 1973.*

ished its fourth album, which, although it was untitled, became known as *The Four Symbols* (after it's runic symbols on the inner sleeve allocated to each member of the group). The third album featured a rotating cardboard wheel inside the sleeve, made to look like an old fashioned seed catalogue as much of the material had been written in a Welsh cottage called Bron-y-Aur in Snowdonia, which Robert had visited with his parents as a child. Jimmy and Robert went off to the cottage for a holiday armed with their

---

'The chemistry between us was immediate and perfect'
ROBERT PLANT

---

acoustic guitars. Said Jimmy, 'As the nights wore on the guitars came out and numbers were written. It wasn't really planned as a working holiday but some songs did come out of it.' One that didn't was the first number on the album 'Immigrant Song', which was much heavier than the Bron-Y-Aur inspired material.

This was put together in the studio, built around a powerful drumming back beat from Bonham. Robert wrote the lyrics for 'Immigrant Song' and most of the album, with the exception of 'Tangerine' and as a whole the album reflected Robert's growing influence on the material with his penchant for romanticism, and acoustic music. Said Robert, 'The great thing about our stay in Snowdonia was there was no motion, just privacy and nature and the beauty of the people there. It was a good experience in every way.'

Jimmy and Robert took tape recorders with them on their walks around the countryside just to make sure if an idea came up it wouldn't go to waste. A typical example of this was 'That's The Way'. Said Jimmy, 'This was written in Wales, when Robert and I stayed at the cottage. It was one of those days after a long walk and we were setting back . . . we had a guitar with us. It was a tiring walk coming down a ravine and we stopped and sat down. I played the tune and Robert sang a verse straight off. We had a tape recorder and got the tune down.'

The sessions for the album, once the material was assembled, were held at Headley Grange, a country house studio in Hampshire. Not everyone was happy with the folksier aspects of Led Zeppelin and their diversion into songs like 'Hats Off To Harper' a tribute to Roy Harper, an artist Jimmy and Robert admired and had met at Bath Festival. Said Jimmy,

● LEFT: *The Power & the Glory.*

● ABOVE: *Mates: John Bonham and Robert.*

● RIGHT: *Plant and John Paul Jones.*

'Our albums were mostly a statement of where we were at the time of recording. But after the second LP which had a lot of hard hitting rock, it (the third album) was interpreted as us mellowing and losing all our power. This album was to get across more versatility and to use more combinations of instruments. We'll never stop doing the heavy things, because that comes out of us naturally when we play. But there is another side to us. The new album (*The Four Symbols*) is totally different from the others and I see it as a new direction. The fourth album should be our best and if it isn't well we might as well give up and retire with red faces. Everybody in the band is going through some changes; there are changes in the playing and in the lyrics. Robert is really getting involved in his lyric writing – and when you get fed up with the LP there is the added pleasure of ripping the cover apart to find out what's on the rest of the wheel!'

Jimmy had planned to experiment still further on the fourth album and intended to have one long track running for about twenty-five minutes featuring mandolin and banjo, as well as the drums and guitars. But when the reaction to *III* was less than ecstatic, there was some rethinking. Said Jimmy, somewhat bitterly, 'The band came under a lot of attack from the press after the third LP. The music press attitude is that you're God one minute and shit the next. So on the fourth LP we decided to release it with nothing on whatsoever, no name of the band, but just the runes and just saying, "This is us, you don't have to buy the LP, so don't if that's the way it is."'

Despite low key presentation, the fourth album contained one particular song that would ring round the world 'Stairway To Heaven', a beautiful, romantic ballad, was sung with tender feeling by Robert, and enhanced by Page's most tasteful acoustic guitar work. This great song crept up on the world, unannounced in March 1971 when the band first performed it during some concerts in Belfast and Dublin. The band arrived in Northern Ireland at a time when 'The Troubles' were at a peak, and violent riots were going on in the streets while the band were playing inside the Ulster Hall. The fans ignored the outside world and gave the band one of the most ecstatic and heartfelt welcomes of their career. They especially appreciated Zeppelin's visit, as so many bands had cancelled trips to the province.

The new song went down remarkably well, even though hard rock fans tended to want to hear the same old fast, heavy riffs. The debut performance was reviewed in the *Melody Maker* and 'Stairway' was described as 'an excellent ballad which displayed Robert's developing lyricism'. Robert was delighted by the cheering response and took the opportunity to tell the Belfast fans: 'A lot of those musical papers that come from across the sea say we

● LEFT: *Rockin' the Irish, at the Boxing Stadium, Dublin, 1971.*

● INSET: *Checking in.*

are going to break up. Well – we're never going to break up!' The fans rushed the stage as Zep roared into their final numbers 'Boogie Mama' and 'Communication Breakdown'.

'Stairway to Heaven crystallized the essence of the band . . .'
JIMMY PAGE

'Stairway To Heaven' was well received everywhere but would take on particular significance in America, where it was played constantly on radio for years and was the signal for fans to light candles (later gas lighters) to express their warmth of feeling. Said Jimmy, 'Stairway To Heaven' crystallized the essence of the band. It had everything there and showed the band at its best. We were careful never to release it as a single. It was a milestone for us. Every musician wants to do something of lasting quality, something that will hold up for a long time, and I guess we did it with 'Stairway'.

The Four Symbols album was released in November 1971 and had been recorded earlier in the year at Headley Grange, using the Rolling Stones mobile truck. Tracks included 'Black Dog', 'Rock And Roll', 'The Battle Of Evermore', 'Stairway To Heaven', 'Misty Mountain Hop', 'Four Sticks', 'Going To California', and 'When The Levee Breaks'. Jimmy described how 'Stairway' was put together: 'There's actually a first rehearsal tape of it, and sixty per cent of the lyrics Robert came in with off the cuff, which was quite something. When we were recording it, there were little bits, little sections that I'd done, getting reference pieces down on cassette, and sometimes I referred back to them if I felt there was something right that could be included.' The song built towards a big climax with John Bonham coming in half-way through the song. 'It was an idea I'd used before, to give that extra kick. Then there's a fanfare towards the solo, and Robert comes in with a tremendous vocal.'

As the song had several guitar overdubs, Jimmy was worried about playing it on-stage. So he got a double neck guitar to help recreate the acoustic backing. Standing ovations, first in Belfast and then later in Los Angeles confirmed the song worked 'live'.

So there was no need for the band to retire with red faces. There was some embarrassment among the record executives who had told Jimmy he and the band were committing 'professional suicide' by putting out the fourth album without their name on the cover. There was no writing at all, just a picture of a hermit with a bundle of rods on his back. Apart from being *The* Hermit, who represents mystical wisdom and self reliance in the Tarot Cards, he also represented man living in harmony with nature. The early seventies were a time for romanticism, searches for lost civilisations and ancient knowledge, and concern for planetary well-being; all destined to be ridiculed by later generations facing the harsh realities of unemployment and the recession. But all that lay in the future. The sun shone bright in the seventies, and poets could dream unabashed.

Even so there were rumblings of discontent and dark clouds on the horizon. For the first three years of their existence, fortune smiled on Led Zeppelin. Apart from a minor car crash involving Robert, life was one long round of awards, accolades and the steady roaring of a torrent of riches. The most they had to worry about was a few bad reviews and the annoying habit some reviewers had of comparing them with Grand Funk Railroad. 'I can't see any comparison,' complained Jimmy, 'It really hurts to be compared to a band which is just about volume. We did acoustic things on our first album which I thought had created a precedent for us. We know where we are going as a group. We are four individuals who have found a common denominator in music. We're getting better all the time!'

In July they played at Vigorelli Stadium in Milan, Italy, and were in for a brutal shock. After a couple of numbers the 12,000 strong audience stood up in a natural response to the music. (Nowadays nobody sits down at rock concerts). The innocent gesture of the fans was misinterpreted by the police and soldiers guarding the stadium. They attacked the fans with tear gas and baton charges. During the subsequent riot the group fled the stage while most of their equipment was stolen or wrecked, despite their roadies' best efforts to save it. The fumes from tear gas cannisters, fired by the police, drifted over the stage and the band had to escape down a tunnel filled with gas.

Next month Zeppelin returned to America for their seventh tour and played twenty concerts which earned them $1,000,000, and they finished off the year with the release of *Four Symbols* and a British tour which included two nights at Wembley Arena (attended by 19,000 people). They were one of the first bands to play at the venue then known as the Empire Pool. It was to be a year before British fans saw the band again as most of 1972 was taken up with tours of America, Australia and the Far East.

A single version of 'Black Dog' from the album was released in America, where it went to No. 15 in the charts. In Singapore they were banned because of their long hair – a fate which also befell Cliff Richard – while doing a tour of Japan the band played a charity show in aid of the victims of the Hiroshima atomic bomb blast.

All the touring meant that work on their fifth album, *Houses Of The Holy* was delayed but it eventually came out in March 1973. Advance orders ensured it 'went gold' even before it was released. The cover was another anonymous affair with no mention of

Zeppelin's name, but instead featured young naked girls clambering up a mountainside. The tracks were 'The Song Remains the Same', 'The Rain Song', 'Over The Hills And Far Away', 'The Crunge', 'Dancing Days', 'D'yer Mak'er', 'No Quarter' and 'The Ocean'.

Once again there were difficult pieces for the band to reproduce 'live' including 'The Rain Song' which had a lot of overdubs. There was even more stylistic diversion with the reggae inspired 'D'yer Mak'er'

● 'Hurry up and wait'. Still in transit; Grant, Page and Jones.

and a curious item called 'The Crunge'

Reviews were mixed, and it would be two years before they released another album. But this was partly because the band had begun to diversify its activities, and taking stock of themselves felt the need to do something about the normal routine of tours and albums.

By now Zeppelin did everything on a grand scale. Their 1973 American tour broke all records and the sheer drawing power of the band mesmerised the music business. Other groups could only stand in awe as Zeppelin rampaged through thirty-three US cities, flying to and fro in their hired Boeing 'Star Ship', grossing a cool $5,000,000. When they played the opening date at the baseball stadium in Atlanta, the mayor proclaimed that Zeppelin were the biggest thing to hit the city 'since *Gone With The Wind*'. The group were towing tons of equipment including special lighting, spinning mirrors, stroboscopes and smoke generators, manhandled by a thirty-strong road crew. They earned $250,000 for the Atlanta show, and went onto draw 56,800 fans to their gig in Tampa, Florida, beating The Beatles' attendance record of 55,000 at Shea Stadium back in the sixties.

It was during this tour that film director Joe Massott began work with his camera crew, filming concerts in Boston, Baltimore and New York's Madison Square Garden. The footage would eventually be included in Led Zeppelin's box office smash hit movie, *The Song Remains The Same*.

It was after the second night at Madison Square that the band were involved in their first serious bout of bad publicity. The Italian riot hadn't hit the national press, but when $180,000 went missing from a safe deposit box at the Drake Hotel, Zeppelin found themselved pursued by TV and newspaper reporters. The money had been takings from their concerts, and

was placed in the safe by their tour manager Richard Cole. The band first heard about the robbery while they sneaked off-stage during John Bonham's drum solo on 'Moby Dick'. Said John later, 'If we'd have said we were not upset they would have thought we were so rich it meant nothing to us, and if we say we're upset about it, they'll say money is all we care about.' The band showed that what they felt was most important, by going back on-stage and finishing their three hour concert.

Perhaps a *Financial Times* report that the band would earn some $35,000,000 during 1973, meant that the New York safe robbery wasn't so important. But the mystery surrounding the identity of the robbers all added to Zeppelin's mystique. The money had been set aside, not for the group, but to pay for the hired Boeing, the film crew and hotels. In the subsequent row Peter Grant was arrested for hitting a photographer, and Richard Cole had to take a lie detector test, which he passed, thus exonerating him from suspicions that he had staged the robbery himself.

By now the band had begun to develop quite a reputation for hell-raising and general 'heaviness'. This was encouraged by a combination of factors.

The Zeppelin camp were keen to make and keep friends with the industry and always treated their fans well. But they reacted angrily towards bootleggers, seizing recording equipment set up during concerts and later organising raids on premises stocking bootleg records or tapes. It seemed odd in view of Zeppelin's huge earnings from record sales and concerts, but it reflected the defensive tactics of men who had to pull themselves up by their bootstraps and weren't prepared to yield even when they had finally reached the top. In fact the band couldn't help but take a sneaking interest in the bootleg i.e. illegal pirate recordings. And with the advent of ever more sophis-

- LEFT: *The young aesthete.*
- ABOVE: *Robert in superstud pose.*
- BELOW: *Coda poster on Sunset Boulevard.*

'Thank you for your time, it's been our pleasure'
ROBERT PLANT

ticated pocket recorders and spread of the ubiquitous cassette, Zeppelin, in common with most other groups were powerless to prevent the practice, which means it is now possible to hear the band at most stages of its development, from the Lyceum concert of 1969 to Knebworth in 1979.

There was Peter Grant's determination that the band should not be put upon or ripped off. Although normally a warm and considerate man, his sheer size and occasionally menacing tone was sufficient to warn people off. And he was not averse to using his old wrestler's dodge of butting the unwise and unwary with his stomach.

Peter Grant's celebrated 'presence' was also helpful when it came to stopping promoters trying to con him over ticket sales, merchandising and the rest. When dealing with thousands of dollars, in cash on a roller coaster ride around the States, there was no sense in presenting a soft target.

The other aspect of Zeppelin's increasingly notorious reputation was their penchant for riotous assembly. Loaded with cash, surrounded by adoring girls and protected from serious retribution, it was no wonder that the chaps often went somewhat over the top. There were fights, orgies, wrecking sprees, inflight hooliganism, heavy drinking and wild pranks. Most of this, however, was centred around their tour manager Richard Cole, in cahouts with John Bonham, who was most prone to stuffing mudsharks in hotel wardrobes (or passing nubiles), riding motor cycles along corridors, dancing on tables and tossing TV sets into pools. Page and Plant were mostly amused spectators during such revels. However Jimmy's avowed interest in magic, the occult and Aleister Crowley, known as 'The Beast', added to his and the band's increasingly overpowering image. There were warning lights flashing. Led Zeppelin seemed like a juggernaut heading for disaster.

Yet Zeppelin were no worse than most other bands confined to hotel and dressing rooms on long tours. 'The road' was a mixture of numbing boredom and incredible highs. There were endless flights and long drives, then adrenalin pumping concerts and all night parties. Wives and girlfriends waited anxiously at home while the menfolk went off on foraging expeditions, rather like eighteenth century soldiers of fortune.

CHAPTER SEVEN

THE PRINCIPLES
OF PLANT

The sudden demise of Led Zeppelin left the surviving members in a state of limbo. For all of them it was obviously a time to rest, but enforced inactitivy for musicians who had been used to working hard for most of their lives was hard to bear. John Paul Jones had less of a problem; he didn't have a public image to live up to, beyond his reputation for sound musicianship. He could carry on with his life and go on making music without a great burden of expectation bearing him down. Page and Plant, however, were idols, their image fixed in the collective memory of a generation. They were faced with many problems. The decision to end Led Zeppelin, however right and proper, left a gaping hole in their lives and they were shattered by the tragic death of their friend John Bonham.

Assuming that one day they would want to carry on performing and making music, what sort of music could they play, and who would want to come and see them? They were assailed with doubts and fears. There was one thing, however, that was clear. Whatever steps they took, they would have to exercise extreme caution. Few artists get a crack at a second career in pop music. They had to avoid rushing headlong into ill considered ventures, but they had to ensure that time didn't pass them by and leave them stranded like beached whales.

There was no shortage of advice from friends, commentators, fans and the record industry, most of which Page and Plant studiously ignored. And in the aftermath of Zeppelin there was no end of rumours, most of which reached the bemused ears of Robert and Jimmy. Plant told how he was in a record store when the shop assistant confidently told him how Led Zeppelin was going to reform with Jason Bonham, John's son, on drums. All this was conveyed without the hapless assistant recognising Robert.

Those who did not expect a Zeppelin reunion, were most intrigued about Robert's chances of a successful solo career. After all, he was the youngest, still retained his good looks, was in obvious good health, and had, so to speak, been stopped in mid-breath by Zeppelin's break up. And whatever bad odour had been caused by some of Zeppelin's more nefarious activities, none of this had wafted over Plant's name.

It was a curious by-product of Zeppelin's success that Robert had been virtually cut off from contact with the music scene at large for many years. Zeppelin were a family concern. All Robert's singing and writing was directed towards the band. Once he had

● *The new Robert.*

fulfilled his commitment there, he was off to the country to live on his farm with wife and children. There was no sitting-in, or recording with other musicians. Any musical decision could only be in conjunction with Jimmy and the rest of the band. Said Robert looking back on his career, 'With Zeppelin it was so comfortable that I never had a thought beyond our records or tours. I was totally consumed by it. Socially it might have been better for me to have met more people.' That was one thing Robert wanted to put right in the months following Zeppelin's end.

When John Bonham died Robert felt right away that Zeppelin had come to the end of the road and there was no point in carrying on with another drummer. If they had got in another player then he would have felt constrained to announce him as a 'temporary replacement' at every gig, which wouldn't have been too pleasant for the drummer. Robert just felt upset and confused by the turn of events and while normally a brash, confident and witty man, he now felt indecisive and weighed down with gloom. For seven months he locked himself away from the world and became a recluse. He realised that one day he would have to come back and start singing and recording again, but he couldn't begin to deal with putting such plans into action.

In any case the great Led Zeppelin organisation seemed to be slipping into decline. With Peter Grant and Jimmy Page out of the picture and Swan Song records being wound down, there were few people Robert could turn to for help. He spent a lot of time just catching up, listening to the radio and to all the old Led Zeppelin albums – perhaps to check out how well they stood up in the light of modern developments.

Gradually Robert recovered from the loss of his friend and began to miss the things that had given shape and substance to his life; the thrill of performing live in front of a responsive audience, and the delight of working with top class musicians constantly pushing each other to greater creative heights. He began visiting small clubs around the Midlands. Even while he was engaged in these tentative ventures, the public were ready to believe that a new super group was being prepared, possibly featuring a combination of talents from Yes (who had also broken up) and Zeppelin. It was suggested in some quarters the band would be called XYZ, meaning Ex-Yes-Zeppelin. Robert dismissed all this as rubbish, but there was a plan afoot to launch a band with Chris Squire (ex-Yes) and Jimmy Page, called Cinema. In the event, Yes reformed, without any assistance from Zeppelin.

Robert had begun working with a band on a loose basis, without any advance publicity or ballyhoo, which eventually became known as The Honeydrippers. Robert vowed he would cancel the gigs if it was announced by eager promoters that he was in the band. It was rather like the tactics used by Paul McCartney when launching Wings in the aftermath of The Beatles. Robert told top British rock writer Steve Gett, 'It was extremely hard for me to even consider working with other people. I didn't want to play with anyone, but then The Honeydrippers sort of got me at it again. We went around England appearing in small clubs. It was great fun to be able to go out and play without any of the usual pressures.'

The first signs of activity were when Robert, then aged thirty-three, teamed up with guitarist Robbie Blunt, Andy Sylvester, and ex-Zeppelin sound man Benji LeFevre. Sylvester played guitar and bass and it was really his band. The Honeydrippers took their name from the one used by fifties' blues star Roosevelt Sykes. Robert's new colleagues were all blues veterans themselves; Andy had played bass with Savoy Brown and Chicken Shack; Robbie had played guitar in Bronco, a group which featured another fine singer, Jess Roden, and with Silver Head and Steve Gibbons' Band.

With Kevin O'Neill on drums, and Ricky Cool and Kevin Davis on saxophones, the band made its debut in Stourbridge on March 9, 1981. They went on to play at all the local clubs and pubs including J.B.'s in Dudley. The existence of the band was barely noticed by the home music press while abroad Robert's old fans were in complete ignorance of his activities. 'It was really an exercise for me to regain confidence and find out if I could still sing. I wanted to get back in front of people, face to face. And I wanted to find out whether I'd got the nerve, or if I had any convictions' said Robert. The band played songs by Otis Rush and B.B. King. They also played Albert King's 'Crosscut Saw', Buddy Holly's 'Tell Me How', and 'Honkey Tonk', the famed Bill Doggett instrumental.

Although the early gigs were fun, tension began to build up when some members of the group, anxious for stardom they had never enjoyed, began to wonder why they couldn't play big theatres instead of the small bars Robert preferred. They were in effect only there to help Robert escape the glare of publicity and Robert began to find playing old blues and rock standards a drag.

The next obvious move was to start writing original material. Robert had known Robbie Blunt for some years and it was natural to form a songwriting partnership with him, as he began to think about the possibilities of recording a solo album. 'Robbie and I had been playing out our rhythm and blues fantasies in The Honeydrippers. But gradually we began to realise the limitations as things got repetitious. So, in between gigs, we started sitting down with a 4-track tape machine, and writing bits and pieces.' In September Robert and Blunt had already started work on the long awaited solo album, recording at Rockfield Studios in Wales. Included on the sessions was Paul Martinez (bass), Gerald 'Jess' Woodroffe (keyboards) and Cozy Powell (drums). The first tracks laid down, with Powell on drums were 'Slow Dancer' and 'Like I've Never Been Gone.' It was hoped that Cozy Powell would stay with the new group but at the time he was committed to working with guitarist Michael Schenker. Robert decided to ask Phil Collins, one of the nation's finest drummers, if he could finish off the sessions. Said Phil later, 'When Robert first asked me to play, I originally said I couldn't because I was working and only had weekends off. But he kind of twisted my arm and so I went down to the studios for three days.' In December 1981 there occured an intriguing ceremony, barely reported at the time, when Robert, Jimmy and John Paul Jones were reunited at the Golden Lion public house in Fulham, West London. They presented an acoustic guitar in a competition planned to raise money for a children's charity.

Robert had completed the process of rebuilding his nerves with the live gigs and was ready for the studio. He explained how The Honeydrippers had helped him. 'It was just being taken as a singer without the pomp and circumstance which came with Zeppelin. If I could do that and enjoy it, I reckoned I could do it on a more dynamic and perhaps inventive level. It was probably more nerve racking with The

Honeydrippers than it was before or after. There were so many possibilities open to me that I couldn't decide right away what to do. So I decided to have fun with The Honeydrippers. I enjoyed myself tremendously but felt it was high time to do some original material. I did not want to lean on the past. That would have been immoral. Robbie and I reached a point where we could write songs together. Although we had known each other for a long time, it was a traumatic experience for me to write with someone other than Jimmy. Page and I were able to work for hours and hours without stimulants, just because we knew that we were giving birth to something.' Robert later admitted that he found it frustrating when he first began to work with different musicians. 'They would be totally exhausted after two or three hours. They'd get headaches, saying ''I have to go out and have a walk around''.'

Robert was also encourged by his mate Cozy Powell to start singing on the session, like he had done in the old days. 'Go on, do all that screaming' he'd yell at Robert. Plant barked back, 'Look, if I feel like it I'll do it, but I don't particularly see that I need to keep throwing in trademarks. The songs are strong anyway, I don't have to lean this way or that. I sing how I sing, that's enough!'

The album, called *Pictures At Eleven* was released in June 1982. The critics approved. Robert was relieved. Zeppelin fans gave two cheers, and contemporary pop fans seemed to extend a welcome to the 'newcomer'.

The next obvious step was to form a regular band

● TOP: *Robert takes a bow, with Phil Collins and band, Seattle, 1983.*

● ABOVE: *Robert with Robbie Blunt, looking oddly Page-like, Newcastle, 1983.*

ROBERT PLANT   DAVE EDMUNDS   JAKE BURNS

● *The surprise come back, on BBC TV's Pop Quiz.*

and go out on the road. But Robert felt he didn't have enough material ready. The last thing he wanted was to put together a Zeppelin type band that mixed old and new songs, even though plenty of singers from his era were doing the same thing, like Steve Marriott, or Ozzy Osbourne. Somehow he thought that would be the 'easy way out' although if the truth be known, most of those singers, successful or not, were having a hard time with their health and nerves. It certainly wasn't easy for them. They had to carry on doing what they knew best.

Unlike those artists who had to relive their past to attract attention, Robert was under close scrutiny and still famous; so *Pictures At Eleven* was crucial to his future. He was delighted with the results. 'I look back on it with a great deal of love', Robert told Steve Gett. 'It was very well done and it was good to work with Benji LeFevre and Pat Moran, the engineers who kept quality control over the whole thing. They were formative days.' Robert wrote the lyrics while Robbie Blunt came up with the chord structures, guitar parts and solos. Nothing was written down, except for the lyrics. All the various tunes and riffs were put down on tape recorders, in the usual sloppy way used by rock musicians who can't be bothered to master the simple skills of reading and writing music.

The sound of the record came as a big surprise. The music was decidedly modern and despite Cozy Powells assertion that it 'sounded like Led Zeppelin' in fact there was little if any resemblance to the old group. 'It's a new strain – alternative hard music is what I'm trying for,' explained Robert. It was Blunt's job to be patient and understand Robert's wild hand

signals and yells which were his only means of communicating the new ideas. 'He's very patient, a good foil,' said Robert. 'I haven't always got a hard and fast line on the music. My role in my band is very similar to my role in Zeppelin, except I can be a bit more adamant. I suppose I have called the tune . . . gently. Everybody is on the same wavelength. They know the point I am trying to get across. Over the years I will continue to make records that will change depending on how I feel. And people will come along because they'll be into that approach rather than playing it safe. It means there's going to be a selective crowd.' Robert hoped that when he finally went on tour there would be intelligent understanding from his audience, rather than a shower of fire-crackers and 'maniac, teeth-gritted, eyes-glaring response.'

All the while Robert was working on his first solo album (which was also his first studio work in three years, first collection of Plant compositions away from Zep and his first production effort), he kept in touch with his old mentor Jimmy Page. 'When I was recording the album I kept taking tapes over to Jimmy to get his opinion. It was very emotional. Like there were times I just wanted to cry or hold his hand. When I played Jimmy the complete album, he knew then that I had gone, was forging ahead alone.'

In fact, while *Pictures At Eleven* sold well and 'went gold' it didn't sell as well as the last Led Zeppelin LP produced by Jimmy Page and released the same year, called *Coda* which racked up a million sales worldwide – one lesson perhaps that Robert needed to learn from Page was the virtue of brevity in production. Robert himself commented, 'When I listened to the first album a lot I realised that it was almost choked with music. Every bar was filled with twelve strings and glittering glockenspiels. It was just too crowded. The album was joyously overdone. Things like 'Pledge Pin' and 'Fat Lip' saved it. So I learned from listening to *Pictures.*'

Many fans missed the vocal histrionics which had been his forte in Zeppelin. Explained Robert: 'I don't do those long vocal waaahs anymore because I don't feel it happening. It depends what day it is as to how well I sing. I think if you sing high it comes over better on radio, if you sing low, it gets lost in the low and bottom end sounds of a record. I just love to sing. It's simple. Most people love to do one thing. I'm lucky because my singing attracts attention. There's nothing particularly profound about me. Most of my lyrics are about boy and girl situations. Being a solo artist is a whole different thing from being part of a group. There are so many decisions that must be made. I must take this responsibility. I can't heap it onto anybody else. In Led Zeppelin, mostly I was out for a good time!' Some wondered if Robert wasn't past his peak now that middle age loomed over the horizon. 'It's no good chasing eternal youth', he agreed. 'But if you're happy in what you do then you don't even think about getting older. I still love music. I've had a good run, and I haven't finished running yet. I don't feel that age has affected my singing.'

Around the time of the release of this first album Robert surprised British fans by making a guest appearance on the popular BBC TV show *Pop Quiz*, sporting short hair and a relaxed manner. He still hadn't done any post-Zeppelin interviews at this point and it was a good way of showing his face without having to face a barrage of Zeppelin related inquiries. Then in June 1982 he went to America for some radio interviews where he was somewhat in the firing line; he had to explain patiently that there wasn't going to be a Zeppelin reunion and that he wasn't ready to tour himself until he had got another album ready.

While Robert was busy re-organising his music career, there were other changes, or a more personal nature. In January 1983 it was reported that Robert and his wife Maureen had divorced. Maureen had supported Robert from the earliest days, Robert had even sung with Led Zeppelin on their wedding night, back in 1968. They had been through a lot together, but now they had separated, on good terms. Robert described their mood during the break up as 'placid' and explained that they had both woken up one morning having realised a 'few realities'. Robert decided to move to London, back to the centre of the music business and relinquished his ten acre farm and life in a cottage. 'I had two dogs, six goats, several ducks and a beer belly. All have gone now. The dogs were wonderful but the goats were a bit of an encumberance.' He went to live in a West London flat, but was able to see his children Carmen and Logan, on a regular basis. Later Maureen would go and see Robert when he finally took the plunge and went on tour. It reminded her of the old days when Robert toured non-stop with Zeppelin. Robert told writer Pete Silverton, 'We still see just about the same amount of each other. All it's done is to remove the

rough edges of a relationship. It's taken off the flashpoints so we can no longer behave any way other than as friends. A lot of marriages are maintained for other purposes. Ours is now a relationship we can boast is OK.'

It was all part of Robert's process of 'coming out' of a web of cocoons, which included his colleagues in Zeppelin, who he admitted, he rarely saw now. 'Emotionaly I haven't drawn the curtains on anybody. You don't create barriers just because a band finishes. But because the band did finish I thought I really had to take myself into a little corner and start afresh. I just felt I'd have a better chance if I made my own decisions, right or wrong. It was time to stand on my own two feet. I had thirteen years of being in one compartment.'

A year after *Pictures At Eleven*, in June 1983, Robert released his second album *The Principle Of Moments* on his own newly formed Es Parenza label, distributed by Atlantic Records. He also released a single, 'Big Log', from the album which got to number one, somewhat inappropriately in the heavy metal charts, and did well all around the world. Said Robert: ''Big Log' was a really good song for every reason. It was more palatable, easier to listen to more and more times which is why it worked on the radio.' Once again Robert had written all the lyrics and the songs were constructed by Robert in collaboration with the band. Ex-Jethro Tull drummer Barriemore Barlow played on two tracks and Phil Collins laid down the rest. Although more accessible and less cluttered than the first album, the new material continued in the same vein – a search for modern, relevant sounds, which Robert delivered with a mixture of restraint and passion.

The new album sold sufficiently to earn Robert another gold record which encouraged him to get back on the road and full scale tours of America and Britain were announced. In late August Robert set off on his first concert tour as a solo artist, something that had been denied him even in The Band Of Joy days. He was committed to a six week journey across North America and it proved to be a triumphant return. He wasn't heckled or plagued with requests for old songs, and the fans accepted the new music he had to offer. The *Chicago Sun Times* reviewed the opening show and said: 'From the high spirits throughout the crowd it was obvious that Plant remains as much beloved on his own as he was with Zeppelin. No one we've seen on tour over the past year drew such a consistently excited response.'

Robert made a special video to promote 'Big Log' which was shown consistently on MTV in America helping the single to reach number twenty in the Billboard chart.

'It was great fun to be able to go out and play without any of the usual pressures'
ROBERT PLANT

Where was it all leading them, and what could they do with all the vast sums being generated? Well there was the taxman to pay, but there were also plans for expansion and in 1974 Zeppelin set up their own record label, Swan Song, with headquarters in London and New York. All the band's subsequent LPs were released on Swan Song, and distributed by Atlantic. Other artists signed to the new label were The Pretty Things and Maggie Bell. A party held in Chislehurst Caves in Kent, to celebrate the release of Silk Torpedo by The Pretty Things was hailed as one of the highlights of the year, once the hangovers had worn off.

Meanwhile work on 'The Song Remains The Same' continued and extra 'fantasy' sequences were shot to showcase each member of the band – Joe Massott started the work on these but was later replaced by another director. These 'fantasies' were forerunners of the pop video which became such a feature of the 1980s. John Bonham was shown driving a drag racing car during his drum solo, Robert rescued a fair maid from a castle, John Paul Jones scared local yokels as a masked night rider and Jimmy climbed a steep hill in search of The Hermit.

Jimmy filmed his episode on the shores of Loch Ness near Boleskin House, the property which once belonged to Aleister Crowley, and which Jimmy bought in 1970. It was all part of Page's on-going interest 'in magick' which had begun at school. He collected many of Crowley's manuscripts and books and many claimed that Jimmy himself had become a 'magician' through his studies. As an apparently shy

young man, who never spoke to audiences, but could exercise great power over them through his music, the concept of magic and its gifts of inner strength and independence must have been most appealing. After all, music and the different emotions and reactions it arouses, is arguably a form of magic with good and evil aspects.

Jimmy would talk quite freely about his interest in Crowley in the early days of Zeppelin. And much of his obsession with things magical and mystical would become apparent in Zeppelin artwork, particularly on the *Houses Of The Holy* album, with its gatefold picture of naked beings offering themselves up for sacrifice upon ancient rocks in front of a ruined castle. But it would be hard to read any great significance into the lyrics, despite constant claims of secret black magic messages. There is nothing particularly devilish about 'Sing Out Hare Hare, dance the Hoochie Koo, city lights are oh so bright, as we go sliding through,' ('The Song Remains The Same'), or 'She's the kind of girl makes me jump and shout', ('The Crunge'). Doubtless many such lyrics were the result of Robert improvising in the studio, rather than any attempt to make direct communications with Lucifer, the Old Gentleman, or the Arch Fiend himself.

Increasing speculation, particularly in the American music press, about Page's interest in magic, led to the supposition that he was arousing unseen forces which were acting against the group. Certainly there was a run of bad luck which began to plague the band, and a combination of illness, tragedy and violent incidents began to tarnish their image and weaken the power and prestige they had built up with such assiduous labour.

Mentally and physically the team were overtaxed and overstretched by hard living, over indulgence and endless tours. This combination, rather than any form of mumbo jumbo, made them more susceptible to the slings and arrows of outrageous fortune. The band themselves decried any talk of a 'curse' as being offensive and nonsensical.

In 1975, half way through the decade, Led Zeppelin were at the peak of their popularity, and they celebrated this by playing five nights at London's Earls Court exhibition centre. They presented their full American production, and it was the first, and perhaps last time. that a generation of British fans saw the band. Those who had missed them in their formative years were in for a treat. The band were magnificent and the music on their new double album *Physical Graffiti* was sensational.

The year began with Jimmy catching his finger in a train door at Victoria station and he thought he might not be able to play for months. But the digit healed and the show went on. Jimmy took pain killers and dropped difficult numbers like 'Dazed 'and Confused' from some of their dates. Their 1975 US tour started on January 18 and carried on until the end of March. Once again the band travelled by 'Starship' around the States and concerts sold out within hours of tickets going on sale; there was a riot among fans queueing for tickets in Boston and their show was cancelled; more riots followed in Greensboro, North Carolina; and tickets for their shows at Madison Square Garden and Nassau Coliseum sold out within thirty-six hours – America was gripped by Zeppelin fever.

The band played five songs from *Physical Graffiti* during their three hour marathon show. They used lasers, a 70,000 watt PA system and a 300,000 watt lighting rig complete with revolving mirrors. It was rock's finest hour.

The album went gold and platinum as soon as it was released in March. Tracks included 'Custard Pie', 'The Rover', 'In My Time Of Dying', 'Houses Of The Holy', 'Bron-Y-Aur', 'Down By The Seaside', 'Ten Years Gone', 'Night Flight', 'The Wanton Song', 'Boogie With Stu', 'Black Country Woman' and 'Sick Again'. Not all the tracks were brand new, some had been recorded years before, but had not been included on previous albums. The two outstanding tracks were the menacing Eastern flavoured 'Kashmir' and the funky 'Trampled Underfoot'. Recalled Jimmy when discussing the album with John Tobler: 'The intensity of *Kashmir* was such that when we'd done it, we knew that it was something so magnetic you just couldn't describe what the quality was. It was just Bonzo and myself at Headley Grange at the start of that one. He started the drums and I did the riff and the overdubs, which get duplicated by an orchestra at the end, which brought it even more to life. It seemed so ominous. It's nice to go for a mood and know you've pulled it off.

'*Physical Graffiti* was the longest album to make because we had about three sides of the new material recorded and it seemed to be a good idea to put on some of the numbers that had been left off previous LPs. With 'In The Light' we knew exactly what its construction was going to be, but nevertheless I had no idea at the time that John Paul was going to come up with such an amazing synthesiser intro, plus there were bowed guitars at the beginning to give a drone effect.'

Physical Graffiti went straight to the top of the American charts and all six Zeppelin albums showed up in the US Top 200. The band were justly proud of the album and Robert Plant explained how it was put together; 'It was a case of getting together and feeling out the moods of each of us when we met up in the studio for the first time in six months. We began as always, playing and fooling around for a couple of days, including our own standards. Slowly we developed a feel which took us into the new material. Some of the stuff came directly from this approach like 'Trampled Underfoot' and some came from Jonesy or Pagey or myself – seldom myself – bringing along some structure which needed working on.'

While the new material was encouragingly successful, most American and British fans still wanted to hear Robert sing 'Stairway To Heaven'. Said Robert, 'It's quite a moving thing . . . hearing 20,000 people singing along to 'Stairway To Heaven'. People leave satisfied after that. This was our most successful tour on every level. The music gelled amazingly well. Everyone loved *Physical Graffiti* and that meant a lot. We were on an incredible winning streak. It's not just that we think we're the best group in the world. It's just that we think were so much better than whoever is Number Two.'

When the band finally came home to play at Earls Court the same fever pitch excitement was generated in Britain. There were 100,000 postal applications for tickets and extra shows had to be put on. During five days of concerts, 85,000 saw the band playing their hearts out. Few who saw the shows would forget the sheer excitement and spectacle of the event; green laser beams cut through clouds of smoke engulfing Jimmy Page as he produced an eerie howl of violin bow against guitar strings; and a huge projection screen displayed full colour close ups of Robert and

● *Unpack, put the kettle on . . .*

Jimmy strutting their stuff. Bare chested and clad in tight denim jeans, Robert epitomised the macho cocksure rock singer, laughing, joking and screaming out the lyrics to a succession of classic songs. Page appeared in a black velvet outfit, a stage suit, embroidered with gold dragons. He stalked the stage, eyes closed, hair cascading over his face, lost in the emotions generated by the musical forces they unleashed.

They began their Earls Court shows with 'Rock'n-'Roll' and worked their way through 'In My Time Of Dying', 'Kashmir', 'No Quarter', 'Tangerine', 'Trampled Underfoot', 'Moby Dick', 'Dazed And Confused', 'Stairway To Heaven', 'Whole Lotta Love' and 'Black Dog'. During 'Love' Jimmy brought into play a giant wand which produced weird noises as he made magical passes over it with his hands. It was the final act in a thrilling musical drama. Rather significantly Robert told the crowd on the last night, 'Thank you for your time, it's been our pleasure. We'll see you again, maybe in the 1980s'.

It was suspected that the band were planning to live abroad due to heavy taxation imposed by the Chancellor, Denis Healey. Indeed they had a lot of work lined up abroad as well as various holidays, but none of the group actually took up permanent residence abroad.

Following the triumph at Earls Court, the first of a succession of hammer blows struck the group, from which they never fully recovered. While on holiday with his family on the Greek island of Rhodes, Robert was involved in a serious accident. His hired car hit a tree. Mrs Plant suffered a fractured pelvis and skull, and Robert had multiple fractures in the ankle and elbows. Their two children Karac and Carmen sitting in the back seats, were unharmed. Maureen was concussed for thirty-six hours and Robert had to be airlifted home for treatment. Their world tour was cancelled and Plant eventually flew to Malibu, California, to recover.

Jimmy flew out to see him and they decided that they might as well use the period of convalescence to record. The result was *Presence* an album recorded at Musicland in Munich, Germany and released on Swan Song in April 1976.

Robert slowly recovered from his injuries and even felt strong enough to sit in with a bar band while on a visit to Jersey in the Channel Islands with John Bonham. He had recorded the album whilst on crutches but was able to walk unaided once more by the New Year. Although the new album wasn't up to the block busting standards of *Graffiti*, it contained one especially powerful piece 'Achilles Last Stand'. The other items were 'For Your Life', 'Royal Orleans', 'Nobodys Fault But Mine', 'Candy Store Rock', 'Hots On For Nowhere', and 'Tea For One'. It was all done in three weeks, and one of the songs, 'Tea For One', reflected Robert's loneliness at being separated from his wife and kids due to the combination of tax laws and the accident. Recalled Jimmy, 'When we were doing *Presence* we made an attempt at a blues that

was called 'Tea For One' about ultimate loneliness in a hotel room'. Jimmy had to play a blue solo in the middle of the tune and was somewhat daunted by the fact that every guitarist in rock from Eric Clapton onwards had played every blues lick known to science. 'So what was I going to do?' mused Jimmy. 'It was one of the last solos to go on because I'd feared it. But it had this atmosphere to it, and when I heard it back, I was really pleased with it.'

Meanwhile controversy still surrounded the band. The actor Telly Savalas, who played *Kojak* in the popular TV series complained of their rudeness towards him on a flight across the Atlantic. And underground film maker and magic person Kenneth Anger, complained bitterly that Jimmy Page hadn't finished writing music he had promised for his film *Lucifer Rising*. Jimmy responded that Anger hadn't finished the film.

In the autumn the film *The Song Remains The Same* was premiered in New York and London. Critics attacked the film for being egotistical and suggested that the soundtrack was no longer truely 'live', as the Madison Square recordings on which it was based had been cleaned up in the studio. Certainly there was rather a flat sound about the 'live' double album from the film released in October, and containing all their most famous songs.

There had been considerable uncertainty about Zeppelin's future after Robert's car accident. But by the beginning of 1977 the band were ready to tour the world again, and take on the newly emergent punk rock bands, spearheaded by the Sex Pistols. A great music business backlash had begun to hit established bands like Zeppelin who were overnight deemed 'dinosaurs' or 'boring old farts'. Punk gave dissidents the excuse to fight back at what was seen as the overpowering weight of bands that had been around too long, and whose wealth in particular put them outside the experience of ordinary kids facing the growing perils of unemployment. Capitalism was a dirty word, and statistics and technological skills meant nothing. The primeval scream of the Pistols, Clash and Damned seemed to cut through the edifice of rock like wire through cheese.

Naturally Led Zeppelin didn't see themselves as 'dinosaurs' and indeed publicly embraced the new movement by going to see the bands in action at some of London's nefarious punk clubs. They compared the bands to themselves when they had their first toe on the ladder. Then in April 1977 Led Zeppelin began their eleventh tour of the States which was planned to be their biggest ever. They were due to play fifty-one concerts in thirty cities, playing three hours a night, and using video screens at the larger venues. On April 30 they played to 76,229 fans at the Pontiac Silverdome, the largest audience for a single band in rock's history thus far.

The tour would come to a sudden halt in tragic circumstances. Curiously enough, earlier in the year the American magazine *Circus* had suggested that Zeppelin were on a 'karmic collision course' and claimed there was some strange force at work attempting to prevent Zeppelin touring America. Their run of bad luck, culminating in Robert's car crash was cited, along with various other minor accidents and injuries. While playing at the Chicago Stadium Jimmy suddenly sat down in the middle of 'Ten Years Gone' and the concert was abandoned after an hour. It was the first time Zeppelin had ever had to stop a gig. 'We always have a go, really,' said Jimmy later, 'because we're not a rip off band. But the pain was unbearable. If I hadn't sat down, I would have fallen over.' It seemed he was suffering from food poisoning. However he was soon back on the road, smoking endless Marlboro cigarettes to sooth his nerves.

The band completed the first leg of the tour and returned to England to receive an Ivor Novello award for their contribution to British popular music, and take a short holiday. They went back to the States in June. Their concert at Tampa, Florida was stopped by a thunderstorm, and although the band promised to return the next day, there was a minor riot. Zeppelin completed six sell-out nights at Madison Square Garden. The wild reaction showed that as far as most rock fans were concerned Led Zeppelin were world beaters.

Perhaps the accolades and riches had gone to their heads. At any rate the band's entourage including John Bonham, Peter Grant, Richard Cole and a security man became involved in a fracas with staff employed by promoter Bill Graham, backstage at the Oakland Coliseum. A minor dispute sparked off the fight which resulted in arrests and criminal charges for assault. Neither Jimmy, Robert or Paul Jones were involved. There was worse to come. A few days later on July 26 a message was flashed from England to say that Robert's five year old son Karac had fallen ill with a stomach infection. His condition worsened and he was taken to hospital but it was too late. He was dead on arrival by ambulance. Robert flew back to England and the rest of the tour was cancelled. Back home in September John Bonham was involved in a car crash near his home and broke two ribs. The headline in *Rolling Stone* magazine pronounced gloomily: 'The wrong goodbye. Led Zeppelin leaves America'.

Jimmy Page began a series of interviews to put the record straight about the band and it's future. He angrily denied they were breaking up and refuted all talk about 'karma'. Said Jimmy, 'It really shocks me that people could write that about the band. The whole concept of the band is entertainment. I don't see any link between that and karma, it's all nonsense . . . a horrible, tasteless thing to say. And I don't see how the band would merit a karmic attack. All I have attempted to do is go out and have a good time and please people.' He thought all the bad luck that had hit the band was due to 'coincidence'. Asked if he believed someone had put a curse on the band he replied 'I can't account for the lunatic fringe'.

The band retired from public gaze for a few months

● *Facing the future, US tour 1983.*

and Jimmy used the time to write new songs and sort out old tapes. Early in 1978 the charges against the Zeppelin team mates involved in the fight came to court in California, in their absence the men were fined and received suspended sentences. It seemed unlikely they would be made welcome in the States for a long while.

In May the band reunited, for the first time in ten months, at Clearwell Castle in the Forest Of Dean to begin making music again. 'It seemed like an eternity' said Jimmy. Shortly after Robert made his first public appearance singing rock'n'roll tunes like 'Blue Suede Shoes' as Melvin Giganticus with the Turd Burglers at Wolverly Memorial Hall near his Worcestershire home. More jam sessions followed including a gig with Dave Edmunds at Birmingham Odeon. It was all designed to get Robert used to performing again, although some suspected it showed a desire to start building a solo career outside of Led Zeppelin.

The call of Zeppelin remained strong, and in 1979 it was announced that the band would play concerts at Knebworth in Hertfordshire. First they played two warm up shows in Copenhagen, then returned to England for their first Knebworth performance on August 4, when they were supported by Chas and Dave and Todd Rundgren. On August 11 they were supported by Keith Richard's New Barbarians.

Zeppelin showed a determination to 'edit' their

• House Full. Odeon, Hammersmith.

• Roadies raffle at Golden Lion, Fulham. John Paul,
Robert and Jimmy back together for presentation.

performances at Knebworth perhaps to avoid some of the accusations of overkill that has recently been levelled at them. They cut out John Bonham's full length drum solo, and the guitar solos were shorter. John Paul Jones played much more piano and Robert sang with all the power he could muster. The roars of applause greeted 'Stairway To Heaven' and 'Trampled Underfoot', but the audience whilst attentive seemed constrained, and Robert showed signs of being upset by the lack of wild fervour which they had come to expect, particularly in America. They were however playing to many newcomers, intermingled with the faithful. They seemed more curious than fanatical, and at some moments you could hear a pin drop as the 100,000 strong crowd stood in silence. They had waited a long time to see the band and they weren't quite sure how to react. It was their last chance to see the legends. A year later, John Bonham died and Led Zeppelin broke up.

All's fair in love, war and rock'n'roll, but Led Zeppelin didn't deserve the abuse heaped on them in national and music papers after Knebworth. Some said they had 'squeezed their lemons dry', while others called them 'the worst band in the world' (the New Barbarians being hailed as an example of 'the best'). All this was really a reaction, or groundswell of resentment from those who perceived Led Zeppelin as a consistent threat to the establishment of a new order. Even so the bulk of rock fans remained loyal to Led Zeppelin and its music, and their 1979 album *In Through The Out Door* released in August, went to the top of the US charts. It was number one there for weeks, although sales were not as good at home. The band even released a single in America from the album, 'Fool In The Rain' backed with 'Hot Dog'.

In April 1980 the band began rehearsing in London for a European tour, and they intended returning to America for the first time since the disasters of 1977. It was rumoured that the band were not in good shape. They had played a few dates in Germany when John Bonham collapsed in Nuremburg after three numbers. He was soon back for the rest of the dates. Although some thought their performances were rough and ready compared to the slick precision of yesteryear they displayed good humour and enthusiasm as they blasted through 'Black Dog'. Jimmy wore a baggy white suit and Robert was in his favourite denim jeans.

Jimmy expressed himself well pleased with their playing and confirmed that a nineteen date tour of North America would begin in Canada on October 17. There was a wild rush for tickets. Then came the last shattering blow. On Thursday September 25 John Bonham was found dead at Jimmy Page's new home in Windsor. He had been drinking vodka heavily over the previous twelve hours. At the inquest held on October 8 it was stated that he had died as a result of suffocation from inhaling his own vomit while asleep, the same fate that had befallen Jimi Hendrix. Friends believed the heavy drinking bout had been sparked off by personal problems and anxiety about the impending return to America, where there had been so much ill-feeling on their last trip. John's funeral was held in a parish church in Rushock, Worcestershire, on October 10, a few miles from his farm. Tributes poured in with many top drummers expressing their sadness at his passing and admiration for his contribution to music.

Speculation began as to who would be likely to replace John Bonham in Led Zeppelin; Cozy Powell, Carmine Appice and Peter Cross of Kiss were among names bandied about. Eventually the group put an end to all the rumours with a brief statement issued by Swan Song to the leading news agencies.

It said' 'We wish it to be known that the loss of our dear friend and the deep sense of undivided harmony felt by ourselves and our manager, have led us to decide that we could not continue as we were.'

There was to be no further amplification of this statement, except later Jimmy confirmed they couldn't really carry on as Led Zeppelin without Bonzo. Soon it became apparent that the remaining members would drift apart and commence solo careers. All hope of a reunion gradually faded as first, Robert Plant and then Jimmy Page began to make their mark with their own bands and albums. The story of rock'n'roll is full of twists and surprises, but no one in the winter of 1980 (the same month that John Lennon was shot dead) could believe that one day the remnants of Led Zeppelin, most celebrated rock band of all time, would one day come together and play 'Whole Lotta Love' and 'Stairway To Heaven' just one more time.

At last Robert had a large enough bag of material to make full scale concert touring feasible. The full list of songs included on the first album were 'Burning Down One Side', 'Moonlight In Samosa', 'Pledge Pin', 'Slow Dancer', 'Worse Than Detroit', 'Fat Lip', 'Like I've Never Been Gone' and 'Mystery Title', while the songs on The Principle Of Moments were 'Other Arms', 'In The Mood', 'Messin' With The Mekon', 'Wreckless Love', 'Thru With The Two Step', 'Horizontal Departure', 'Stranger Here . . . Than Over There', and 'Big Log'.

Fans were somewhat puzzled by the use of obscure song titles. But it was explained that 'Horizontal Departure' referred to their bass player Paul being carried horizontally out of a pub, and 'Big Log' was simply a smoking log on an open fire which drove the band away from one of its camp fire sing songs. (And if you believe that you'll believe anything). It reached fifteen in the U.K. singles chart and Robert was quickly invited to make his first appearance on BBC TV's Top Of The Pops. Both albums and single made healthy progress in the American charts and Robert's appearances on MTV for interviews and a 'Big Log' video all helped. The album sold better as the band began its journey across the States. Tickets went on sale on July 5 and most sold out quite rapidly.

Robert wasn't going back to larger venues completely 'cold'; in July 1982 he had sung at London's Dominion Theatre at a Rock Gala concert in aid of the Princes Trust, which was later made available on video; and in May he had jammed on-stage in Munich at a Foreigner concert with Jimmy Page, for a hectic version of 'Lucille'. In August 1983 Robert went to Dallas, Texas to carry on rehearsals with his band, begun earlier in Shepperton Studios in England. The band included Robbie Blunt (guitar), Paul Martinez (bass), Jezz Woodroffe (keyboards), and new members Bob Mayo (guitar/keyboards) and Ritchie Hayward of Little Feat on drums for the British dates and Phil Collins for the American Leg.

The American tour dates were Rosemont, Chicago (August 29), Arena, Milwaukee (31), Arena, Detroit (September 3), Coliseum, Cleveland (4), Worcester, Mass (6), Forum, Montreal (8), Auditorium, Buffalo (9), Maple Leaf Gardens, Ontario (10), Madison Square Garden, New York (12), Hartford, Connecticut (13), Spectrum, Philadelphia (14), Coliseum, Memphis (16), Baton Rouge (18), Summit, Houston (20), Centre, Austin (21), Arena, Dallas (22), Arena, Denver (24), Forum, Los Angeles (27), Coliseum, Oakland (28), Coliseum, Seattle (30) and Coliseum, Vancouver, (October 1).

The band opened each show with 'In The Mood' and

'I've had a good run, and I haven't finished running yet'
ROBERT PLANT

invariably played; 'Pledge Pin', 'Messing With The Mekon', 'Worse Than Detroit', 'Moonlight In Samosa', 'Fat Lip', 'Thru With The Two Step', 'Other Arms', 'Horizontal Departure', 'Wreckless Love', 'Slow Dancer', and 'Like I've Never Been Gone'. The encore numbers chosen were 'Big Log', 'Burning Down One Side', 'Little Sister' and 'Stranger Here . . . Than Over There'.

The burning question was how would American fans react to Robert's new 'rock'n'roll for the eighties?' The testing time was the split seconds after the end of 'In The Mood'. The crowds cheered, and Robert could rest assured he had last been accepted as an artist in his own right and he could step out from the shadow of Zeppelin.

When the band walked out onto the stage at Madison Square, scene of many past Zeppelin triumphs, there was a five minute standing ovation before Plant's new chums had played a note. A significant portion of the New York crowd were wearing their old Led Zep teeshirts and it was clear they loved Robert as a Zeppelin hero, and were ready to honour him whatever his new band sounded like. Although he wouldn't play any old Zeppelin numbers, it was those songs stylistically closest to Zep like 'Slow Dancer' which went down best . . .

Rock critics generally approved, and noted the absence of long improvised solos, beyond the 'freak out' routine in 'Stranger Here . . .'. They thought the band sounded restrained and precise rather than wild and emotional. Wrote one U.S. reviewer: 'The raw emotion and ability to take chances that was Zeppelin's forte, was certainly not evident on this tour. The new band are a much more staid group of chaps. Although they're all excellent musicians, none of them have quite the charisma or talent to go down in history on the level of a Jimmy Page or a John Bonham, or for that matter, even a Robert Plant. But Robert's success in 1983 is certainly well deserved.'

There were no disasters on the tour, beyond one cancelled date in San Diego, caused when one of the equipment trucks broke down, and most of the tickets were sold.

The British tour began at the Apollo, Glasgow, on November 22, 1983, and the rest of the dates were Playhouse, Edinburgh (23), Empire, Liverpool (25), University, Leeds (26), City Hall, Newcastle (28), City Hall, Sheffield (December 1)), Coliseum, St Austell, Cornwall (3), Colston Hall, Bristol (4), Gaumont, Southampton (6), Gaumont, Ipswich (7), Apollo, Manchester (9), Odeon, Hammersmith, London (12), Top Rank, Cardiff (14), Centre, Brighton (17), Apollo, Oxford (18), Royal Centre, Nottingham (20), De Montfort Hall, Leicester (21), and Odeon, Birmingham (23).

After the British dates the band were due to travel on to Japan, Australia, New Zealand, Hong Kong and Bangkok. The British tour went very well although the local critics were less generous than the Americans. One of the highlights of the U.K. trek was the Odeon Hammersmith show when Jimmy Page came on-stage for a brief jam session.

One U K reviewer, Tom Gibbert writing in *Smash Hits* described Robert as 'one time singer with hoary heavy metal group Led Zeppelin,' and said he had 'acquired a suitably modern looking band . . . for Robert is deter-

● *Robert breaks the media ice.*

mined to bury the past.' He felt that the songs were 'loud, long and slow, based around Plant's high pitched echo treated screech, several clanking guitar solos, and harmonic dramatics in a minor key. An occasional stab at white reggae or a segment of Arabian caterwauling cannot disguise the fact this is essentially a very old fashioned sound, designed primarily for American adult orientated radio. It is highly slick and professional. It is also more than a trifle dull.' Hibbert thought Robert was more like a country and western singer than a rock star, because of the friendly and chatty way Robert introduced the numbers.

Other critics however raved about the band and paid tribute to the superb drumming of Richie Hayward, and the 'exhilarating and inventive' guitar work of Robbie Blunt. Robert's singing was praised, in particular on 'Like I've Never Been Gone'. When Robert was reunited at the Odeon Hammersmith with his old sparring partner it caused great excitement. Wrote Mark Storey in *Music* magazine: 'The unexpected but much dreamed of appearance of Jimmy Page was a sight worth seeing. The fact that he actually plugged in a Gibson was nirvana. The result was total euphoria as Hammersmith erupted to 'Treat Her Right.' '

After the world tour, Robert kept a low profile throughout the rest of 1984, emerging at the end of the year with a surprise package, a ten inch LP called *The Honey Drippers Volume One*. Complete with simplistic cover showing black and white shots of sax and trumpet players and a James Dean lookalike, it was an attempt at recreating the Fifties spirit. It was recorded in New York at Atlantic studios with Jeff Beck and Jimmy Page popping up for some fairly unrecognisable guitar solos. The mini-LP was released in December and tracks included 'I Get A Thrill', 'Sea Of Love', 'I Got A Woman', 'Young Boy Blues' and 'Rockin' At Midnight'. 'Sea Of Love' was released as a single backed with 'Rockin' At Midnight', and a video was made to accompany the record. The former featured Robert wandering around a seaside setting, apparently serenading a pair of bobby soxers (including the James Dean lookalike), while the old Roy Brown song 'Rockin' At Midnight' was illustrated with a montage of old dance clips, intercut with Robert posing like Elvis.

The material was poles apart from the serious, modernism of his first two solo albums, and was intended as light relief. And yet it didn't quite work. The band was very slick, if strangely stiff. 'Rockin' At Midnight' tried too hard to be authentic. The Beck/Page cameos were rather wasted, as they could have been any old session players, and the strings on 'Sea Of Love' were greeted with alarm by those who still cherished memories of Robert the bare chested Viking. Another technical problem, was that the ten inch LP wouldn't play on the latest front loading record players, Japanese technology having deemed such discs obsolete.

Nowhere was the anguish and confusion aroused by the LP more evident than in the pages of *Hot Led* a Led Zeppelin collectors newsletter circulated among British fans. Proprietor, editor and chief critic Luke Barr (aged 14), expressed his disappointment by heading his LP review 'Honeydrips'. Wrote Luke: 'We waited and we anticipated, but was it worth it? Plant and Pagey, back with Beck? WOW! But then the doubts started to flood in . . .'. Luke proceeded to disparage the guitar solos as 'not particularly good', claimed his stomach churned at the sound of 'I Get A Thrill', and complained bitterly about 'Sea Of Love' and its strings. 'Appalling intro . . . straight out of Muzak for supermarkets. As for 'Young Boy Blues', to unearth all these relics is just not on. Not for ex-Led Zeppelin rock superstar super-sexy vocalist Robert Anthony Plant. And 'Rockin' At Midnight' . . . they obviously enjoyed recording it because Robert laughs.'

A normal size version of the record was released as well, but sales were not dramatic. Snapped Phil Carson, at the time head of Atlantic Records in London, in answer to criticism: 'It's meant to be fun . . . remember fun?'

The problem was the fun of The Honeydrippers and all it meant to Robert with his long term love affair with rock'n'roll and the blues, came across much better 'live' than it did on record, ten or twelve inch varieties. Ironically, because The Honeydrippers were beginning to become better known, it was now harder to do the anonymous 'secret gigs' of the early eighties. So in January 1985 Robert got together with his old mates to perform under the name of The Skinnydippers. and played a superb concert at the Rolls Hall Hotel, Monmouth, Wales.

It was an extraordinary evening, with the audience reacting, strongly to the old rock standards. Robert was amazed at the ease with which he could communicate. In fact he hardly stopped talking between the numbers, chatting about the origins of the songs, and Leon Russell and Ben E. King and offering potted histories of the stars.

When the crowd cheered and sang along to a solemnly performed version of 'The Young Ones' it prompted Robert to say: 'And that's all it takes . . . after all these years of sweating, all these years of pulling faces and all these thoughts about what we should do on *The Tube* and whether we're recording the right or wrong music, and all you've gotta do is go round to places like this, play Cliff Richard songs, and it'll all be okay!' A loud cheer greeted this breathless, revealing speech, followed by shouts from two giggling Welsh girls for 'Summer 'Oliday'! After another rap, about The Drifters' early use of violins, then a spot of tuning up, a voice at the back bellowed 'Come on, get on with it'. 'What do you expect for nuthin'?' chided Robert. 'Stairway to 'Eaven', giggled the girl in the front row. But Robert counted in 'Save The Last Dance For Me' and rocked on regardless, showing himself hugely competent with a warm tone, good pitchings and all the other attributes of a 'real' singer that many thought didn't exist beneath the screaming exterior of the Zeppelin years.

Robert made plans to combat the problem of establishing himself as a contemporary artist with original things to say, while leaving himself room to enjoy 'good time' music. In the summer he released his latest album *Shaken 'n' Stirred* produced by Robert and Benji Lefevre and assisted by Tim Palmer. It was another powerful, modern set of songs, which were to be featured on his 1985 American tour which began on June 10. The album was recorded at Rockfield studios with Blunt (guitar), Martinez (bass), Woodroffe (keyboards) and Hayward (drums). The new songs were beefed up with the violent attack epitomised by the electro pop of the previous year. Tracks were 'Hip To Hoo', 'Kallalou Kallalou', 'Too Loud', 'Trouble Your Money', 'Pink and Black', 'Little By Little', 'Doo Doo A Do Do', 'Easily Led', and 'Sixties and Sevens'. As well as playing selections from these songs on the tour Robert also featured a section with The Honeydrippers, using horns and three girl back-up singers. They played 'Rockin' At Midnight', 'Sea Of Love', 'Young Boy Blues' and Big Joe Turner style rave up.

The back-up singers were also featured on the *Shaken'n'Stirred* material, and 'Kallalou Kallalou' was chosen as the encore number. But it seemed most of the US critics were not enamoured with the new songs and only liked the Honeydrippers' section of the shows. Fans however were delighted by the spectacle of Robert leaping around the LA Forum 'like a man of twenty years of age,' according to one source.

Meanwhile, back home, it was announced that Robert would play two major shows, at the Birmingham National Exhibition Centre, on September 8 (a massive venue, normally only filled by the likes of Genesis and The Who) and London's Wembley Arena on September 10.

Robert talked about the contrast between his contemporary work and his hankering for 'the good old days' in an interview with *Sound Check* magazine. 'The solo work is the complete opposite to the Honeydrippers, in writing, application and musicianship. We work for hours and hours on new songs, while with The Honeydrippers, if you try it more than twice, and it's not right, you can't do it again . . . you have to say "That's no good, forget it . . . next!"'

Robert answered those who felt that Jeff Beck could have brought more to the forefront of the Honeydrippers' session. 'Well Beck played a lot in 'Rocking At Midnight', all of it in fact. His playing is incredible . . . It's not guitar orientated music, if it had been, I'd really have been treading old ground. What I wanted to do was bring out that element of 'good time' music. The Honeydrippers is a labour of love . . . doing something like 'Sea Of Love' which is a ballad with strings, is tongue-in-cheek. I've never been in a position to do something like that. I like 'Sea Of Love'. I've got three versions of it by Del Shannon, Marty Wilde, and the Phil Phillips and The Twilights original. 'Sea Of Love' is the kind of song I would never have dreamed of recording

seriously in 1980 but suddenly I was in a studio laughing and really having a good time with girls singing.' Many people thought he was crazy to record the song but he did it, 'for a laugh, with real string arrangements.'

Robert seemed prepared to admit that his first two albums, while important, were somewhat hard to take in terms of their heavy, soul searching feel. '*Pictures At Eleven*' was such a trauma, working with different people. It was a weird beginning and *Principal Of Moments* was another step away from everybody still asking for 'Stairway To Heaven'. This is the first opportunity that I've had to play what I want without it immediately being compared to 'Black Dog'. *Principle Of Moments* was a period of my life when I was telling myself I had to go off at a tangent, to get away from the past, and I was trying to be too clever for my own good. The construction of 'Messing With The Mekons' was over the top, with all the pauses, the gaps. There was no room for gigantic guitar solos. There had to be no indulgences. Whereas now it's one . . . two . . . BANG!'

Robert felt proud of his achievements during a five year solo career, but nagging doubts about his musical direction remained. Then slap in the middle of all his plans came the sudden surprise Led Zeppelin reunion, the event they said could never happen. It took Bob Geldof and the historic Live Aid concert held simultaneously in America and Britain, in July 1985 in aid of Ethiopian Famine relief, to bring them together.

Phil Collins played a segment at Wembley, then flew by Concorde across the Atlantic in time for another performance in the epic show which was broadcast around the world by satellite. Phil played a few numbers at piano and then said he would like to introduce 'a few old friends'; out came Robert Plant, Jimmy Page and John Paul Jones. With Phil and another drummer helping out, they launched into rousing, emotion charged versions of 'Rock'n'Roll', 'Stairway To Heaven' and 'Whole Lotta Love'. There had been no rehearsal. They were rough and ready. But the crowds gave the biggest cheer of the entire concert, which had already seen some other historic reunions including Crosby, Stills & Nash and Black Sabbath with Ozzy Osbourne.

The immediate result of this success was a spate of rumours including a story in the London *Daily Mirror* that Led Zeppelin would reform for one more album and a few concerts. What were fans to make of these developments? At the beginning of August a spokesman for Atlantic Records said they were 'seriously considering' the idea. Robert and Jimmy had done a lot of productive work in their years apart, but the cheers and overwhelming demand for a reunion from the fans seemed very hard to resist.

CHAPTER EIGHT
JIMMY PAGE FIGHTING BACK

Jimmy Page was knocked sideways by the events of 1980. Led Zeppelin was his creation, his life, and the main plank of his existence. There had been growing cause for concern about the state of Jimmy's health for some years. Now he seemed in danger of collapse, physically and mentally. The shock of John Bonham's death in his own home, was sufficient to shatter his nerves. If Robert Plant had felt badly about what happened, Jimmy was in an even worse state of confusion.

Apart from his family life (which he has always kept private), he had his own Sol Studio, built by engineer Gus Dudgeon, at Cookham in Berkshire. Here Jimmy would spend many hours engrossed in his own projects and working with friends. Among those who visited the studio at various times were Mick Fleetwood, Bill Wyman, Elton John and George Harrison. For a year Jimmy remained hidden, a reclusive figure, the subject of constant speculation. Then on March 10, 1981, he made a surprise guest appearance at the Odeon Hammersmith with Jeff Beck. He was introduced by Jeff as 'my old school pal.' Jimmy ambled on stage, with a cigarette dangling from his lips to jam with Jeff on 'Goin' Down'.

In answer to incessant questions Jimmy offered some thoughts on his post-Zeppelin future. 'Obviously I really want to get out and play. I'd like to get a vehicle. a group of guys who will provide a

● *Jimmy back on-stage with The Firm, US tour, 1985.*

vehicle for that, and that's the new project, sometime in the New Year.'

It would be four years before Jimmy finally came out with a new band. In the meantime he built up his confidence, not with a regular jam band like The Honeydrippers, but with odd assignments, occasional sit-ins and guest appearances. There were more traumas, like a drugs bust, and the subsequent bad publicity. Also, the largely hostile attitude of the home music press to anybody who had been making records any longer than a week did not help his peace of mind, or offer encouragement.

It seemed like a veil of secrecy had descended over his life and it took the concerted efforts of disparate groups of friends to help him rebuild his career. One of the first to help was his London neighbour, film director Michael Winner. He liked and admired Jimmy and invited him to his home to see his latest film *Death Wish II*. After discussing the merits of the film, which Jimmy liked, Winner hinted that he would like Jimmy to write the music for the film. Michael then told him he had eight weeks to do the job. Said Jimmy; 'I walked out of his house after having had a very pleasant afternoon, feeling like a sledgehammer had hit me over the head. I had eight weeks to do forty-five minutes of music.' The bits of music, some only a few seconds long, required new skills and disciplines, which Jimmy, working with video cassettes, had to learn overnight. Jimmy had to write everything off the cuff, and he said later; 'It was an absolutely incredible exercise in discipline which was

● *Jamming with Roy Harper, Cambridge Folk Festival, 1984.*

terrifying, but I just about made the deadline.' Jimmy used synthesisers extensively, for the first time, on the soundtrack, which was remixed from mono and issued in stereo on an album, *Death Wish II.*

In between recording the soundtrack at Sol he took up a variety of pursuits, from snooker to cricket. And to show there were no hard feelings between him and Robert Plant, the pair took part in the celebrated Munich jam session with Foreigner. Despite the reception they got, Jimmy came to feel that his time as a performer was past and began to fear that audiences, raised on a new breed of pop groups, and used to modern sounds, would not want to see an ageing guitar hero.

In December 1981 Jimmy was arrested in the Kings Road, Chelsea after some cocaine was found in his jacket pocket. He faced a jail sentence, but in October 1982 he was given a conditional discharge at the Inner London Crown Court and ordered to pay £100 costs. His defence lawyer had explained that Jimmy was launching 'a new rock group' and planned to tour America and Japan. If he wasn't discharged he would be automatically banned from both countries which would have a 'catastrophic effect on his future.'

It was a long while before the phantom band emerged. There were the rumours of super groups with Chris Squire of Yes, and the only information that could be gleaned were some vague thoughts on Jimmy's plans from Robert Plant; 'Jimmy's been working on a number of musical projects in his own studio. He has a wonderful studio and he seems totally immersed in music. I can't divulge exactly what he's working on, but from what he's told me it sounds very interesting and exciting. It may be a bit of a departure from what fans may expect but with Jimmy I'm sure it will be fascinating.' When Jimmy could be tracked down, he confirmed; 'I'm looking forward to playing in public again. Music is so much part of me that when I don't play I feel part of my life is missing. I want to get it back.' As Robert had played Jimmy the tapes of his first solo album, Page returned the compliment by going to see Robert's first British tour and then offering to get up and play during Robert's show at Bristol.

A useful product of Jimmy's time in the studio was the album *Coda*, the last Led Zeppelin LP, released on Swan Song, in November 1982. Jimmy had often talked about producing a double LP of archive Zeppelin material in chronological order. This wasn't quite it, but it proved an interesting exercise. The tracks were 'We're Gonna Groove', 'Poor Tim', 'I Can't Quit You Baby', 'Walter's Walk', 'Ozone Baby', 'Darlene', 'Bonzo's Montreaux', and 'Wearing And Tearing'. The first track was a Ben E. King song dating from 1969, and 'Poor Tom' was a sort of nursery rhyme rap from 1970 with Robert singing over a John Bonham shuffle beat. 'I Can't Quit You Baby' was performed superbly by the band at the Royal Albert Hall in 1970. There were a couple of outtakes from the Polar Studios session in Stockholm, which had resulted in the *In Through The Out Door* album, and an electronically treated drum solo featuring 'The John Bonham Drum Orchestra'.

It was strange that Jimmy had achieved less in the three years after Zeppelin than he and the old group had in the first few months of existence. The pace of events had slowed dramatically and it seemed that such a swift rate of development could never be repeated. This didn't mean Jimmy was destined to fade away. Eventually he pulled himself up by the guitar strap and relaunched his career with a convincing flourish.

The impetus was a unique series of charity concerts featuring an all star line-up of British rock stars. One of the music scene's most popular characters was bass player, singer and composer Ronnie Lane. The cheery, talented Londoner had come to fame with the Small Faces in the Sixties. Later he was an integral part of The Faces with Rod Stewart. Ronnie went on to form his own band and attempted many adventurous projects including a travelling rock circus called The Passing Show. Then he became seriously ill with the incurable disease multiple sclerosis. Unable to work, he had to spend his dwindling resources on treatment. It was then that friends rallied round with the idea of a charity concert to raise funds for research into the disease and to help Ronnie out.

The result was two memorable nights at the Royal Albert Hall in London in September 1983. A massive line-up of familiar faces from some of the most famous groups of all time joined together. There was singer Andy Fairweather Low from Amen Corner, Stevie Winwood, ex-Traffic, Bill Wyman and Charlie Watts from the Rolling Stones, and guitarists Eric Clapton, Jeff Beck and Jimmy Page.

When Jimmy Page ventured forth on-stage, with cigarette smouldering, a roar went up. He launched into themes from *Death Wish II* and then delighted his his fans by playing an instrumental version of 'Stairway To Heaven'. Clutching a Fender Telecaster and clad in a grey striped suit over a green vest, he lurched around the stage, swaying with the music. The first piece was 'Who's To Blame' from *Death Wish II* followed by 'City Siren' and 'Prelude'. Then out came the double neck Gibson for 'Stairway To Heaven'. Simon Phillips came in on drums and gave Jimmy solid support. Clearly nervous, he smoked incessantly and his fingers often had difficulty finding the right notes. Nevertheless he produced one of the most emotion packed performances in the annals of rock. It was virtually a one man lament for Led Zeppelin and all that had happened to them.

The hall's pipe organ was brought into play to add to the atmosphere wth a spot of Chopin. Among the guitars Jimmy used on this first full scale public appearance were a sunburst Gibson Les Paul Standard, a black Danelectro, two Telecasters and the red Gibson SG 6/12 string double neck. It was sad that while Jimmy was performing, a thief, ignorant of the fact that he was invading a charity event in aid of the sick, broke into the dressing room and stole Jimmy's Seiko metronome,

some records and even the set list. Later Jimmy joined Clapton and Beck in a rocking jam, all three standing shoulder to shoulder and trading riffs. Watching with approving gaze were the Prince and Princess of Wales. It was over all too soon, but plans were announced for more concerts, this time in America.

The ARMS shows (Action and Research for Multiple Sclerosis) were held in Dallas, San Francisco and Los Angeles before going on to Madison Square Garden in New York City. The music was properly organised and rehearsed. It was the sort of event fans dreamed about in the sixties but could never happen due to clashing egos. Now all were friends and colleagues, united in the desire to help an old mate. Ronnie Lane was there too, singing 'Goodnight Irene' and finding it hard to believe he was being backed by some of the greatest names in rock music. Among them were Joe Cocker, Ron Wood, Bill Wyman, Andy Fairweather Low (slightly out of place but invited at the behest of show organiser Glyn Johns), Chris Stainton, Simon Phillips, Kenney Jones, Charlie Watts, Ray Cooper, Clapton, Beck and Page.

During Jimmy's spot on the American shows he invited singer Paul Rodgers to join in, an event which would take on greater significance some months later. Jimmy knew Paul from the days when Bad Company were signed to Swan Song. Now they found they could get on, and wrote songs together in dressing rooms on the ARMS tour.

● *Ready to rock.*

● The Firm approach.

The wild reaction of American fans to the concerts gave Jimmy a tremendous boost and he began working more extensively this time with another old friend, singer and composer Roy Harper. Jimmy and Roy began recording an album and they also began to make surprise live appearances together. One of these was at the annual May Tree Fair held in Thetford, Norfolk. On a wet Sunday in June 1984 'The Special Band' that had been billed turned out to be Harper and Page, with Jimmy using the pseudonym, James McGregor. Jimmy sporting a brown leather jacket, played 'Highway Blues' and '20th Century Man'. It was revealed that Jimmy was recording with Harper on Roy's 24-track studio in Lytham St Annes. In August they played at the Cambridge Folk Festival with a full band featuring Tony Franklin on bass guitar, Nik Green on keyboards and Steve Broughton drums. They played a beautiful song called 'Elizabeth' and some more powerful pieces like '20th Century Man'. Their album called *Whatever Happened To Jugula* was released by Beggars Banquet on their Second Sight label in 1985. Roy and Jimmy appeared together on *The Old Grey Whistle Test* BBC TV show, where they were seen singing on a Welsh hillside and strumming their guitars. There was a bit of a clash between the presenters and artists; the former claimed the stars were behaving like grumpy old hippies and Roy and Jimmy thought they were being 'set up'.

The important thing was Jimmy Page was getting his guitar 'chops' together again. The long lay-off and incarceration in the studios meant that his once fleet fingers had become slow and stumbling. He seemed incapable of constructing the fast, coherent solos of devastating power that had been such a feature in the past. It was no wonder Jimmy sometimes appeared nervous or defensive. He was in the position that many star instru-

mentalists of the jazz era found themselves, when their reputations outshone failing technique.

But Jimmy hit back at those who scorned his generation of players. Soon rumours suggested that he was about to form his own band with singer Paul Rodgers. In fact rehearsals were going ahead at Nomis Studios in Shepherds Bush. Tony Franklin, the good looking young bass player who had started out with Roy Harper had been invited to join after his impressive performance at Cambridge, and, after much searching Chris Slade, who has played with everyone from Tom Jones to Manfred Mann, was brought in on drums.

The new band was called The Firm. Rumours became fact – Jimmy Page was back in business. A debut LP was recorded and plans made for a world tour. With Phil Carson taking care of the management, Page was ready to go, and the first appearances were in Europe in December 1984. There were no more desultory acoustic guitar duets or hesitant versions of 'Stairway'. Jimmy was determined to go the whole hog and bring back many of his most famous trademarks. And so when he played warm up dates in Sweden and Germany, the fans saw Jimmy Page playing with the violin bow surrounded by blazing green laser beams. It was an unabashed return to showmanship and rock'n-'roll, just what the fans had been waiting for.

Jimmy, like Robert, was keen to introduce some new sounds to his repertoire and with Paul Rodgers produced 'Radioactive', a stomping pop hit, taken off the album and released as their debut single, together with Jimmy's first ever video.

I met Jimmy in Frankfurt and he told me about the formation of The Firm, the making of the album and how fans had helped him get over a crisis in confidence. It was good to see the man who had appeared so uncertain at the first ARMS concert back on form and playing a storm.

The Firm had a problem selling tickets at first, as no one in Copenhagen or Frankfurt seemed to know who was in the group, But once word spread that it starred Paul Rodgers and Jimmy Page then the fans came flocking. The Frankfurt show was at the Kongress Halle which was filled with German and American kids. Paul Rodgers came bouncing on in red shoes and heavily embroidered black shirt. Tony Franklin, in black leather, blond hair flying, proved to be a dextrous bassist, whose solos sometimes threatened to steal the show. Jimmy wore a white satin suit, but soon stripped off the jacket to get down to work.

The band opened up with 'Closer' the first track off *The Firm* which wasn't actually released until February 1985. At Frankfurt they followed up with 'City Sirens' from *Death Wish*. The remaining material was divided between Firm songs, stuff from Paul Rodgers' solo album and some pop standards.

Paul was no Robert Plant, his vocal style was completely the opposite, relying on a warm, understated tone, and deep blues feeling, rather than screams and yells. But he showed that his voice could be a foil to Jimmy's guitar lines, just as Plant had been all those years ago. Paul also played some lead guitar and piano. Jimmy jammed a cigarette between his lips as he rocked back on his heels and stomped through the various riffs. He kept the solos brief, constructing them in a peculiar, cliffhanging sort of way; unpredictable even on the blues. But he could pick our some simple notes that sent shivers down the spine. The band gelled most effectively as a unit on 'Radioactive', and then it was time for Jimmy to turn in a full length guitar workout on 'The Chase' an instrumental that also showcased Tony Franklin and Chris Slade. Both men played their hearts out so when it came to Jimmy's turn there was no

chance that he could slink in the shadows. He had to PLAY! Smoke clouds wreathed around him as laser beams formed a visible cone through the haze. Jimmy held up his violin bow and began creating those magical effects that had stunned the rock world from Madison Square to Earls Court and Knebworth. As the familiar battle cry of 'Wah, wah, wah!' echoed through the hall you could feel the crowd shudder.

Paul Rodgers returned to sing 'Boogie Mama', and the final encore number Solomon Burke's 'Everybody Needs Somebody To Love'. The band faded the number out leaving the audience singing the lyrics, dancing and cheering. As the house lights went up the band threw their arms around each other. Whatever the future might hold, it was as happy a come back as Jimmy could have wished for.

The next day I met Jimmy in the bar for a chat. He sipped whiskey and ice and seemed relaxed and pleased with the turn of events. It was his first interview since the end of Led Zeppelin. Most of the press had been barred from meeting him after one newspaper headlined the advent of The Firm as 'Dead hippies in wake'. The fact that Jimmy Page had never been a hippie, a breed who existed in the years 1966–67, sometime before the advent of Led Zeppelin, and was in a band who had absolutely no connection with the midsixties psychedelic West Coast scene, was a mere technicality.

Jimmy explained that the liason with Paul during the

● *Page and bass ace Tony Franklin.*

ARMS shows. 'We went to the States and had a very good tour and at the end I asked if he fancied carrying on with it and doing something else.' Jimmy emphasised that he didn't want to lose the momentum created by the charity shows. 'I thought "If I stop now I'm just a bloody fool." I had to carry on but the only vehicle I had was playing with Roy Harper and with Ian Stewart (of the Stones). I really wanted to get a band together with Paul and thought some fantastic things could happen. I played on some Alexis Korner cancer benefits with Ian as well as the ARMS things.'

Alexis Korner, the father of British blues, died in January 1984, and Jimmy played an extraordinary concert as a tribute to Alexis in the summer. It took place at the Listoia Blues Festival in Italy. Jimmy found himself teamed with Ginger Baker and Jon Hiseman on drums, Dick Heckstall-Smith, (saxophone), Barbara Thompson (flute), and Georgie Fame (keyboards). Due to heavy rain the band were three hours late on-stage but they played 'Train Kept A Rollin' and 'Sunshine Of Your Love,' a rare treat for a handful of Italian fans.

After this interlude Jimmy had gone back to London to continue rehearsals with Paul Rodgers at Nomis. The band was rumoured to be called The Mac. Jimmy explained why there had been so much secrecy; 'I didn't want it to come out until it was really together. There were lots of rumours but the band wasn't ready. After Paul came down and liked Chris, Tony came in and it was got together very quickly. We just wanted to have a go and play on-stage. One of the first numbers

• *Paul Rodgers trades guitar licks with 'The Guvnor'.*

we played was 'Bird On The Wing' which I wrote with Paul and was quite a test.'

The debut of The Firm was held up for some months because Chris Slade was on tour with Dave Gilmour. Said Jimmy; 'I was playing with lots of people anyway just to keep myself going. After the ARMS thing I thought "I'm not going to stop playing now. I want a group." I did a lot of jams and everyone was invited to come down. Drummer-wise it went from Rat Scabies to Bill Bruford. Then Chris came back again and was brilliant. Tony was on the dole before he joined us and had never played a bass solo on-stage. He's a star now!'

Although Jimmy was pleased with The Firm, he wasn't totally convinced it would last as a long term career. 'Well it started out as a one-off project but now we've seen how it's gone down, who knows?.' 'I've got so many projects. That Ronnie Lane thing did me the world of good. You can't imagine. It gave me so much confidence. Well I realised people DID want to see me play again. So I thought, blow it, I'm not going to let things slip now. I wanna get out there. The business aspect is a bore, but the music is fun.' In the aftermath of Led Zeppelin did he feel he had lost contact? 'I just felt really insecure. Absolutely. I was terrified. I guess that's why I played with Roy whenever I could because I knew his stuff and knew him well.'

The Firm was in total contrast to the music he had played with Roy Harper at the Cambridge Folk Festival, and Jimmy agreed. 'Yeah, it's rock'n'roll, isn't it? I love rocking and having a dance. The rock music I learnt from was always exhilarating stuff. Whenever I feel miserable I put on some old rock'n'roll and feel so much better. It makes the adrenalin rush. Roots music always has that effect on me. When I play a gig it's there for the moment, a thrill lost in time . . . unless it's bootlegged! The idea is to show people who have had a lot of faith in me that I'll go out and have a go. Believe me a lot of fans touch your heart. Especially on the ARMS tour. I realised the fans wanted me back.'

Jimmy confirmed that the old Swan Song label was no more. Some of its artists, like Maggie Bell, were quite bitter about the way it folded. Said Jimmy; 'It was a shame. The idea behind it was good. I know Robert felt bad about it, and I did too. At one point it had the momentum to do a lot, but it didn't.'

Jimmy had enjoyed getting together with Robert Plant on The Honeydrippers LP and he didn't rule out working with him in the future. But many were still intrigued by what Jimmy had done in the months after Led Zeppelin split. 'Well I just didn't know what to do. I lived in a total vacuum. I didn't know what I was doing. In the end I went to Bali and just thought about things. And I wasn't sitting on the beach because it was the rainy season! I sat in my room thinking. Then I thought, dammit, I'm going to do The Firm and see if it works. At this time in my life I should really just do what I enjoy. It involves many different projects and this is just what I enjoy. Some of them are going to be pretty bizarre. I can still rock'n'roll even if everyone thinks the other things are rubbish. I used the violin bow again in the The Firm

● *Heavy solos are back in!*

because it's fun and I know everyone in the audience enjoys it. They're not thinking "What's that wally doing?" It's a light-hearted, tongue-in-cheek thing. Showmanship is great. I've always gone to concerts to be entertained. So lasers and playing the violin bow, all helps out. And playing with Eric Clapton and Jeff Beck in ARMS was great. Brilliant. If only we had more time! It was very emotional when I played 'Stairway To Heaven'. I assumed Jeff Beck was going to come out and help me by playing the melody. But he didn't come on. I've got the double neck guitar on, and everyone is assuming I'm gonna play 'Stairway' so I was really in it. I just had to go for it! I saw the video afterwards and saw my face all screwed up, My God. But I was playing for my life. It kicked me up the ass in more ways than one.'

Jimmy didn't want anybody to sing the lyrics of 'Stairway' and insisted; 'Nobody can sing it but Robert. It wouldn't be right. I did write the music for it, so I could play it. But what stuff did I have? I only had *Death Wish 11*, I didn't have a solo career like everybody else on stage at the Albert Hall. I didn't think there was anything wrong with playing 'Stairway' as an instrumental. There were a few cock-ups but it was alright. I don't regret having done it. I just wish the last gig in New York had

been videoed. That was really happening. If it had happened in the sixties there would have been so many egos flying round. But it wasn't like that. We were just a spearhead for Ronnie. If it had been a package tour it wouldn't have worked with those three guitarists. It was wonderful to be part of it and good things happened for everybody afterwards.'

I asked Jimmy what he thought of Robert's solo career thus far? 'It's been good. He established his identity. His stuff is definitely NOW. It's great and good for him because it's what he wanted to do. The music on the *Honeydrippers* is going back to the kind of Rhythm and Blues we all used to play and that's quite a paradox really. I see Robert a lot and we talk a lot and we're good mates still.' Would they like to work together again in the future? 'Oh sure, I wouldn't have done the Honeydrippers thing if I had felt bitter about it. Sure I'd love to work with Robert again but God knows what sort of musical vehicle we'd be in. He's great. I know him inside out. That's the point. After all those years together you can't help but know each other inside, otherwise you'd have no sensitivity. When you see his big smile . . . at the end of the day that's what it's all about.'

Jimmy admitted it was a hard task to get across new material with The Firm when so many fans really wanted to hear Jimmy, preferably reunited with Robert, doing all the old favourites. But he had to try and get across new ideas, with his new band. 'Some people say this is professional suicide. But I've always done that sort of thing. It would have been the easiest thing in the world to play old hits from Led Zeppelin or Bad Company. That wasn't our idea. We want to prove ourselves as The Firm. We can't rest on our laurels, even though I love playing 'Stairway'. If ever we do get together with Robert again in the future, I hope to do that number.

'In America 'Stairway' became something of an anthem. It's still played on the radio and that number had lasted for twelve years. It's incredible. If you are a musician the one thing you want to do is leave a mark and create something people relate to. That song is it for me. Professionally I still want to keep on trying to play different ideas and not feel that's ALL people wanna see you for.'

Like Robert with the Honeydrippers, Jimmy had sat in with an obscure band, Ian Stewart's Rocket 88 in Nottingham, unannounced and in his case, unrecognised for some time. 'It was great,' recalled Jimmy, 'because I heard people say "Oh that guitarist wasn't bad," and they didn't know who it was. Do you know that meant more to me than anything in the world? It really did. It was bloody magic. It sounds like I'm blowing my own trumpet, but it's not that. It's just it meant so much to me at that point in time. It helped me put things in perspective.'

How did Jimmy feel about the legacy of Led Zeppelin? 'I'm not ashamed of any of that. Led Zeppelin was magic for me. It was a privilege to play in that band. It would have been wrong for me to go out playing the same material and worse to get a singer to sing all Robert's songs. That would have made me an absolute Philistine. I felt it was morally wrong. I knew that Bonzo wanted that music to go on forever. When I played long solos with Led Zeppelin there was a lot of excitement and I got carried away. Now we play more punchy statements. We keep everything to the point. I used to waffle sometimes in the past . . .! Okay they started calling us demi-gods. Well one thing the critics got wrong. If they didn't think we played with conviction they were damn wrong. Now they say all the seventies bands were absolute nonsense, and didn't amount to ANYTHING and they can't relate to anything we ever did. All we get now is good producers doing super mixes. That's where the state of the art is, production. And then miming on-stage with tapes. What's that all about? That's not what WE were all about. And I'm sure the general public don't want to know about it.

'I don't want to sound nostalgic . . . but I *am* 'cos those times were great for me, just like these times are great for others. These are the formative years for other people. There is a whole new generationm going out on the road breaking up hotel rooms. Now everybody is back in their little boxes, and everyone over thirty is finished, which will be fun when THEY get to thirty by the way. I feel really sorry for people who only ever listen to one type of music.

'When I started playing guitar I got involved in all sorts of music. People listened to everything from Ravi Shankar to Jimi Hendrix. There was traditional music and progressive rock, all being listened to at the same time. I thought it was such a brilliant time. As a musician, I thought it was magic. I hope in the future things will get better. I feel disappointed about the way the scene has changed, but who am I to say? People put me down for what I've done in the past. So I'm waiting for them to be a bit adventurous.'

Page denied there would be any more post Zeppelin album releases based on material from the vaults. 'There is some great live stuff, but there's also some great live bootlegs, ha, ha! Thank God they are there and thanks to the people who send me these things. I listen to them and go "My God, that was good, I wish it had been recorded on the line." Because our performances changed so much through all those years it shocks me sometimes to hear what happened.

'Oh it was a privilege that band, the sort of thing everybody dreams about, no matter who they are, a bank manager even. They want to be part of something like that in their own field. For me it was such an honour and that's the only way I think of it. I always thought that John Bonham was the most underrated musician ever. Who else could get so much volume playing from the wrists? I used to try playing with small amps and I just couldn't be heard because he got so much power out of his drums. It's amazing. As he got bigger and bigger kits I had to get bigger amps.'

'I think we have all done it right up to now, Robert, myself and John Paul Jones who has been writing film music and classical pieces. I always wanted to keep in contact with John and Robert and the only way you can really do it is by not talking on the telephone but by playing, even if it's just jamming on a concert or playing on a track that isn't used. That's the only way I can communicate properly, through music. I might live in a bubble but I still get around. I want to prove there is life in the old dog yet. It's as simple as that. I want to enjoy life.

'Sometimes physically and mentally I think "I'm not gonna get through this set," but I do you know, I used to play three hour sets every night with Led Zeppelin. But I don't think I could get through that now.'

When Led Zeppelin stopped in such tragic circumstances did he feel he didn't want to tour ever again? 'No never. Once I came off the road it was such a major part of me missing and I didn't know what it was. It turned out to be having no vehicle to play in. And I had such a reputation for playing live that I got frightened about doing it. If I did four bad gigs nobody would want to know my anymore, and I've got a few more things I want to say in music. People may think "How stupid – what's he talking about?" But it's amazing what you go through.'

'Yes I *am* a musician of the sixties and seventies. I got fired up by the music of Chuck Berry and Elvis Presley. I was hit by so much energy from their records. But every five years people get fired by the music they hear and want to become part of it. So now . . . I'm past middle age. But what do you do when you get to middle age? There was no one for me to look up to who said "This is what you do next." I read in the music press that after thirty you are f****d. But I'm not and there's a lot more for me to do.'

After their European debut The Firm went to America and Jimmy was given a warm reception. They started in Dallas in February, with a triumphant return to Madison Square Garden in April. The single 'Radioactive' was a reasonable hit, and *The Firm* went gold. In May 1985 The Firm played at Birmingham National Exhibition Centre (18), Edinburgh Playhouse (20) and London Wembley Arena (22). Unfortunately the shows were not sell-outs, but at Wembley the crowds cheered as Jimmy struck his familiar poses with the violin bow amidst the laser beams during 'The Chase' and many young fans were given a chance to experience some of the magic of the good old days while appreciating the efforts of a fine new band.

Then in high summer, with both Robert and Jimmy due to tour America with their respective bands, everything was thrown into a state of flux with the Zeppelin reunion in Philadelphia's J.F.K. Stadium for the US Live Aid concert. When Robert, Jimmy and John Paul Jones got back to perform 'Stairway To Heaven' and 'Whole Lotta Love' it seemed like all the barriers to their wishes and desires had been swept away. How a full scale reunion would affect the musicians Plant and Page had been working with over the previous years was open to debate. But there was no doubting the tremendous enthusiasm the simple act of reunion unleashed. However far apart Plant and Page had drifted, powerful forces were bringing them back together. And there was no doubt, a new Page and Plant band, whether they called it Led Zeppelin or no, would solve a lot of problems.

When the crowds are cheering, there is always room for one more encore.

● *Live Aid reunion.*

DISCOGRAPHY

Singles (American Releases Only)

Date	Title	Catalogue No.
March 1969	Good Times, Bad Times/Communication Breakdown	Atlantic 2613
November 1969	Whole Lotta Love/Livin' Lovin' Maid	Atlantic 2690
November 1970	Immigrant Song/Hey Hey What Can I do	Atlantic 2777
December 1971	Black Dog/Misty Mountain Hop	Atlantic 2849
March 1972	Rock And Roll/Four Sticks	Atlantic 2865
May 1973	Over The Hills And Far Away/Dancing Days	Atlantic 2970
October 1973	D'yer Mak'er/The Crunge	Atlantic 2986
March 1975	Trampled Underfoot/Black Country Woman	Swan Song 70102
May 1976	Candy Store Rock/Royal Orleans	Swan Song 70110
December 1979	Fool In The Rain/Hot Dog	Swan Song 71003

N.B.   Trampled Underfoot/Black Country was released in a rare promotional edition in the U.K. in March 1975. 10,000 copies were pressed which now sell at £10 each among collectors. No other official Led Zeppelin singles were released in the U.K.

Albums

Date	Title	Catalogue No.
March 1969	LED ZEPPELIN: Good Times Bad Times/ Babe I'm Gonna Leave You/ You Shook Me/Dazed And Confused/Your Time Is Gonna Come/ Black Mountain Side/Communication Breakdown/I Can't Quit You Baby/How Many More Times	Atlantic K 40031
October 1969	LED ZEPPELIN II: Whole Lotta Love/What Is And What Should Never Be/The Lemon Song/Thank You/Heartbreaker/Living Loving Maid (She's Just A Woman)/Ramble On/Moby Dick/Bring It On Home	Atlantic K 40037
October 1970	LED ZEPPELIN III: Immigrant Song/Friends/Celebration Day/Since I've Been Loving You/Out On The Tiles/Gallows Pole/Tangerine/That's The Way/Bron-Y-Aur Stomp/Hats Off To (Roy) Harper	Atlantic K 50002
November 1971	FOUR SYMBOLS: Black Dog/Rock And Roll/The Battle Of Evermore/Stairway To Heaven/Misty Mountain Hop/Four Sticks/Going To California/ When The Levee Breaks	Atlantic K 50008
March 1973	HOUSES OF THE HOLY: The Song Remains The Same/ The Rain Song/ Over The Hills And Far Away/The Crunge/Dancing Days/D'yer Mak'er/No Quarter/The Ocean	Atlantic K 50014

March 1975	PHYSICAL GRAFFITI:	Swan Song SSK 89400

PHYSICAL GRAFFITI:
Custard Pie/The Rover/In My Time Of Dying/Houses Of The Holy/Trampled Underfoot/Kashmir/In The Light/Bron-Y-Aur/Down By The Seaside/Ten Years Gone/Night Flight/The Wanton Song/Boogie With Stu/Black Country Woman/Sick Again

April 1976   Swan Song SSK 59402
PRESENCE:
Achilles Last Stand/For Your Life/Royal Orleans/Nobody's Fault But Mine/Candy Store Rock/Hots On For Nowhere/Tea For One

October 1976   Swan Song SSK 89402
THE SONG REMAINS THE SAME:
Rock And Roll/Celebration Day/The Song Remains The Same/Rain Song/Dazed And Confused/No Quarter/Stairway To Heaven/Moby Dick/Whole Lotta Love

August 1979   Swan Song SSK 59410
IN THROUGH THE OUT DOOR:
In The Evening/South Bound Saurez/Fool In The Rain/Hot Dog/Carouselambra/All My Love/I'm Gonna Crawl

1982   Swan Song A0051
CODA:
We're Gonna Groove/Poor Tom/I Can't Quit You Baby/Walter's Walk/Ozone Baby/Darlene/Bonzo's Montreaux/Wearing And Tearing

SOLO ALBUMS
Jimmy Page

Date	Title	Catalogue No.

1982   Swan Song SSK 59415
DEATH WISH II:
(The original Soundtrack)
Who's To Blame/The Chase/City Sirens/Jam Sandwich/Carole's Theme/The Release/Hotel Rats & Photostats/Shadow In The City/Jill's Theme/Prelude/Big Band Sax & Violence/Hypnotising Ways

1985 (Feb)   Atlantic 781 239-1
THE FIRM:
Closer/Make Or Break/Someone To Love/Together/Radioactive/You've Lost That Lovin' Feelin'/Money Can't Buy/Satisfaction Guaranteed/Midnight Moonlight

1985   Beggars Banquet BEHA 60
HARPER & PAGE: WHATEVER HAPPENED TO JUGULA?
Nineteen Forty-Eightish/Bad Speech/Hope/Hangman/Elizabeth/Frozen Moment/Twentieth Century Man/Advertisement

SOLO ALBUMS
Robert Plant

Date	Title	Catalogue No.

June 1982   Swan Song SSK 59418
PICTURES AT ELEVEN:
Burning Down One Side/Moonlight In Samosa/Pledge Pin/Slow Dancer/Worse Than Detroit/Fat Lip/Like I've Never Been Gone/Mystery Title

June 1983	THE PRINCIPLE OF MOMENTS: Other Arms/In The Mood/Messin' With The Mekon/Wreckless Love/Thru' With The Two Step/Horizontal Departure/Stranger Here Than Over There/Big Log	Es Paranza 79–0101–
November 1984	THE HONEYDRIPPERS VOLUME I: I Get A Thrill/Sea Of Love/I Got A Woman/Young Boy Blues/ Rockin' At Midnight	Es Paranza 790–220–1
May 1985	SHAKEN 'N' STIRRED: Hip To Hoo/Kallalou Kallalou/Too Loud/Trouble Your Money/ Pink and Black/Little By Little/Doo Doo A Do Do/Easily Lead/ Sixes And Sevens	Es Paranza 790–265–1

SINGLES

Jimmy Page (Sessions)

Date	Title/Artist	Cat. No
1962	**Neil Christian & The Crusaders** The Road To Love In/Big Beat Drum	Columbia DB 4938
1963	A Little Bit Of Someone Else/Get A Load Of This	Columbia DB 7075
	Carter Lewis & The Southerners Sweet & Tender Romance/Who Told You	Oriole CB 1835
	Your Mama's Put Of Town/Somebody Told My Girl	Oriole CB 1868
	Skinny Minnie/Easy To Cry	Oriole CB 1919
	Jet Harris & Tony Meehan Diamonds	Decca F 11563
	Mickie Most The Feminine Look/Shame On You Boy	Columbia DB 7117
	Mickie Most & The Gear Sea Cruise/It's A Little Bit Hot	Columbia 7180
	Mickie Most Money Honey/That's Alright	Columbia DB 7248
	The Redcaps Talkin' About You/Come On Girl	Decca F 11789
	Dave Berry My Baby Left Me	Decca F 11803
1964	**Neil Christian & The Crusaders** Honey Hush/One For The Money	Columbia DB 7289
	Mickey Finn & The Bluemen Pills/Hush Your Mouth	Oriole CB CB 1927
	Pat Wayne & The Beachcombers Roll Over Beethoven/Is It Love	Columbia DB 7182
1964	**The First Gear** A Certain Girl/Leave My Kitchen Alone	Pye 7N15703
	Brenda Lee Is It True/What'd I Say	Brunswick 05915
	The Primitives You Said/How Do You Feel	Pye 7N 15755
	Lulu & The Luvvers Shout	Decca F 11884
	P. J. Proby Hold Me	Decca F 11904
	P. J. Proby Together	Decca F 11967
	Wayne Gibson & The Dynamic Sound Come On Let's Go	Decca F 11800

Brian Poole & The Tremeloes
Candy Man   Decca F 11823
Billy Fury
Aint't Nothing Shakin' But The Leaves On the Trees   Decca F 11888
The Sneekers
Bald Headed Woman/I Just Can't Go To Sleep   Columbia DB 7385
The Zephyrs
I Can Tell   Columbia DB 7199
The Lancastrians
We'll Sing In The Sunshine/Was She Tall   Pye 7 N 15732
Them
Baby Please Don't Go/Gloria   Decca F 12018
The Kinks
You Really Got Me   Pye 7N 15673
All Day And All Of The Night   Pye 7N 15714
The Brooks
Once In A While   London 9668

1965   **Mickey Finn & The Bluemen**
Sporting Life/Night Comes Down   Columbia DB 7510
Jimmy Page
She Just Satisfies/Keep Movin'   Fontana TF 533
Bobbie Graham
Skin Deep/Zoom Widge & Wag   Fontana TF 627
Teensville/Grotty Drums   Fontana TF 627
First Gear
The In Crown/Gotta Make Their Future Bright   Pye 7N 15763
Lulu & The Luvvers
Satisfied/Surprise Surprise   Decca F 12128
The Outsiders
Keep On Doing It/Songs We Sang Last Night   Decca F 12213
Tom Jones
It's Not Unusual   Decca F 12062
Dave Berry
This Strange Effect   Decca F 12188
The Who
I Can't Explain/Bald Headed Woman   Brunswick 05926
David Bowie & The Mannish Boys
I Pity The Fool   Parlophone R5250
The Fifth Avenue
Bells Of Rhymney/Just Like Anyone Would Do   Immediate IM 002
Nico
I'm Not Saying/The Last Mile   Immediate IM003
Gregory Phillips
Down In The Boondocks   Immediate IM 004
The Masterminds
She Belongs To Me/Takin' My Love   Immediate IM 005
John Mayall
I'm Your Witchdoctor/Telephone Blues   Immediate IM 012
Judi Smith
Leaves Come Tumbling Down/Come My Way   Decca F 12132

1966   **The Yardbirds**
Happenings Ten Years Time Ago/Psycho Daisies   Columbia DB 8024
Donovan
Sunshine Superman/The Trip   Pye 7N 17241
Them
Call My Name/Bring 'Em On In   Decca F 12355
Les Fleur De Lys
Wait For Me   Immediate IM 020

Twice As Much		
Sitting On A Fence		Immediate IM 033
Chris Farlowe		
Out Of Time/Baby Make It Soon		Immediate IM 035
Twice As Much		
Step Out Of Line		Immediate IM 036
1967	**The Yardbirds**	
	Little Games/Puzzles	Columbia DB 8165
	Ha Ha Said The Clown/Tinker Tailor	Columbia/Epic 10204
	Donovan	
	Hurdy Gurdy Man/Teen Angel	Pye 7N 17537
	The Yardbirds	
	Goodnight Sweet Josephine/Think About It	Columbia DB 8368
	Jeff Beck	
	Hi Ho Silver Lining/Beck's Bolero	Columbia DB 8151
1968	**Philamore Lincoln**	
	The Wind Blew South	Epic 26497
	Joe Cocker	
	With A Little Help From My Friends	Regal RZ 3013
	Marjorine	Regal RX 3006
1985	**The Firm**	
	Radioactive/Together	Atlantic A 9586

ROBERT PLANT SINGLES

Date	Title	Cat. No.
1966	**Listen**	
	You'd Better Run/Everybody's Gonna Say	CBS 202456
1967	**Robert Plant**	
	Our Song/Laughin' Cryin' Laughin'	CBS 202656
	Long Time Comin'/I've Got A Secret	CBS 2858
1982	12″ E.P.	
	Burning Down One Side, Moonlight In Samosa, Far Post	Swan Song SSK 19429T
	12″ E.P.	
1983	Big Log, Messin' With The Mekon, Stranger Over Here Than Over There.	Es Paranza B 9848T
	Big Log/Messin' With The Mekon	Es Paranza B 9848
	12″ E.P.	
	In The Mood, Pledge Pin (live)	B 6970T
	Horizontal Departure (live).	
	In The Mood/Pledge Pin (live)	Es Paranza B 6970
1985	The Honeydrippers	
	Sea Of Love/Rockin' At Midnight	Es Parenza 7-99701
	Pink And Black/Trouble Your Money	Es Paranza B-9640